A
USER'S GUIDE
TO
COMPUTER
PERIPHERALS

A
USER'S GUIDE
TO
COMPUTER
PERIPHERALS

DONALD EADIE

PRENTICE-HALL, INC., Englewood Cliffs, NJ 07632

Library of Congress Cataloging in Publication Data

Eadie, Donald.
  A user's guide to computer peripherals.

  Bibliography: p.
  Includes index.
  1. Computer input-output equipment. I. Title.
TK7887.5.E22   001.64'4   81-8482
ISBN 0-13-939660-8   AACR2

Editorial/production supervision
  and interior design by *Daniela Lodes*
Manufacturing buyer: *Gordon Osbourne*

Printed in the United States of America
10 9 8 7 6 5 4 3 2 1

ISBN   0-13-939660-8

Prentice-Hall International, Inc., *London*
Prentice-Hall of Australia Pty. Limited, *Sydney*
Prentice-Hall of Canada, Ltd., *Toronto*
Prentice-Hall of India Private Limited, *New Delhi*
Prentice-Hall of Japan, Inc., *Tokyo*
Prentice-Hall of Southeast Asia Pte. Ltd., *Singapore*
Whitehall Books Limited, *Wellington, New Zealand*

Contents

3 LOADING AND UNLOADING DEVICES   40

4 BULK STORE DEVICES   70

5 DISPLAY PERIPHERALS   87

6 COMPUTER INTERFACING   109

10   DESIGNING COMPUTER-BASED SYSTEMS   211

APPENDIX   225

INDEX   237

Preface

The purpose of this book can be summarized as follows:

1. Briefly review the characteristics of peripheral devices which could be considered for use with computer systems of various type and used for different applications.
2. Catalog briefly those devices to be used for newer systems.
3. Indicate the methods and magnitude of the interfacing problem.

This survey is divided into ten chapters. Chapter 1 contains an introduction and a short history, introduces some symbology associated with diagrams in chapters to follow, and includes other general information. Chapter 2 introduces minicomputers and microcomputers. Chapter 3 describes peripherals that load and unload the computer's memory with programs and data. Chapter 4 portrays external peripherals that extend the internal memory of the processor. Chapter 5 covers those devices that allow an operator to view the processing results. Chapter 6 indicates the interfacing problem, describes methods and functions of peripheral control units (PCUs), and describes the relationship between analog and digital systems. Chapter 7 explains the various aspects of digital communication. Chapter 8 describes special systems—that is, when all peripherals are *not* located at a central computer. Chapter 9 defines some of the newer single chip interfaces, fiber optics, etc. Chapter 10 covers the steps that lead to the determinations of new systems and the problems that must be considered. Basics of number systems have been delegated to Appendix A.

Many thanks to those that supplied photographs, permissions, and data—including Reston Publishing Company, Inc., for providing much material from my other book, *Minicomputers—Theory and Operation*; thanks to the reviewers, and those that encouraged me, including R. W. Lowery of Smith Industries, Inc., and D. V. Wilson of Honeywell, Inc. I am especially indebted to my editor, David Boelio, Prentice-Hall, Inc., who saw the need for this book, and for his help and encouragement in so many ways. I would like to thank my wife, who helped me in numerous ways—including help with spelling and getting some xerox copies at critical times.

Donald Eadie

A
USER'S GUIDE
TO
COMPUTER
PERIPHERALS

1

Introduction
and History

1-1 INTRODUCTION

In this chapter we introduce the subject of computer peripherals by first defining what is meant by the term *peripheral*, followed by one method of classification of such devices.   Then a brief history of computers and associated gear precedes comments on basic computer organization, an introduction to logic elements and blocks, interfacing, maintenance, choosing peripherals, and finally a summary of the material covered.

1-2 DEFINITION OF A PERIPHERAL

The computer processor, its logic, and internal memory perform at speeds amounting to millions of operations per second.   To use a computer, an operator, or process, must slow down a computer to a few operations per second, or at most to a few operations per millisecond.   That is the job of a peripheral, in general terms: namely, to

communicate between a device (the processor) working at tremen-
dously high speeds and doing considerable calculating in microseconds
to electromechanical equipment operating at considerably slower
rates. Such peripheral devices may be a printer or a tape reader or a
display cathode-ray tube (CRT) being observed by a technician. The
processor may control an automatic factory process or perhaps an aircraft in flight or the operation of a weapons system. All of these,
insofar as the processor is concerned, are peripherals. In other words,
all equipment which permits one to review the results of computations
visually or to control some process automatically by a processor is a
peripheral. In any event, additional equipment performs the connecting
process, and such equipment is known as *computer peripherals*, the subject of this book. As mentioned previously the following sections
acquaint the reader with some of the basics, such as the possible classifications, diagrams, and definitions of logic symbols, a brief history of
computers, and other assorted topics. This book does not deal in depth
with logic; thus a reader interested in that subject is advised to consult a
detailed book on that topic. The same is true for details on programming although an example of programming in the language BASIC is
provided in a later chapter.

1.2.1   Further Readings

Klingman, E., *Microprocessor System Design.* Englewood Cliffs, NJ: Prentice-Hall,
    Inc., 1977.
Eadie, D., *Modern Data Processors and Systems.* Englewood Cliffs, NJ: Prentice-
    Hall, Inc., 1972.
Eadie, D. *Minicomputers: Theory and Operation.* Reston, VA: Reston Publishing
    Company, Inc., 1979.
Veronis, A., *Microprocessors: Design and Application.* Reston, VA: Reston Publish-
    ing Company, Inc., 1978.

1-3   CLASSIFICATIONS

There are, of course, a variety of ways in which a particular device may
be classified. In this book we have chosen the following approach.
Chapter 2 discusses minicomputers and microcomputers to which
peripherals are attached. Chapter 3 covers devices that load or unload
either data or programs into or out of a computer. Chapter 4 concerns
bulk-store devices, which in general back up the internal memory of a
computer with additional storage capacity. The next chapter treats the
classification of display peripherals, which includes printers, plotters,
cathode-ray tubes, and the like. The object here is to display results
directly to the observer without further processing. Chapter 6 describes

methods for tying computers to peripherals and vice versa. Chapter 7 covers some aspects of digital communication, including a description of some of the equipment, transmission methods, data links, etc. Chapter 8 discusses special systems and some of the newer microcomputer buses now under consideration as possible standards. The next chapter covers briefly some of the newer devices such as one-chip interfaces, fiber optics, and others. In Chapter 10 we conclude with a consideration of what one must do to design a digital system. Number systems and codes are included in Appendix A. With the rapid advance of microcomputer techniques, it is almost impossible to imagine where the future will lead us, especially when one considers that a small circuit card now replaces the largest machines of the 1950s, 1960s, or 1970s. How advances will proceed is a subject of much speculation and debate.

1-4 A BRIEF HISTORY

The earliest device qualifying as a digital calculator is the abacus (sometimes called a *soroban*). This calculation aid, invented about 600 B.C., permits the positioning of beads on a rack. Simple addition and subtraction can be carried out rapidly and efficiently by appropriate positioning of the beads. The abacus is still widely used in the Orient; and its proficient users calculate with great speed.

The first mechanical adding machine was invented in 1642 by Blaise Pascal, a French customs official. Baron Gottfried Wilhelm von Leibniz invented in 1671 the first calculator for multiplication. It is still being developed to this day, but emphasis has shifted almost entirely to integrated circuit designs.

The father of the modern computer is considered to be Charles Babbage, a nineteenth-century professor at Cambridge University. He proposed to the British Admiralty the construction of a differential engine and was given funds and directed to proceed in 1823. In 1833 he started, on his own, the development of an analytical engine and worked on it until 1842. Neither of these devices were successful, mainly because of hardware shortcomings at that time. However, his efforts established a number of fundamental principles for the design of digital computers. Even scientists at Harvard studied his work before embarking on the Mark 1 effort in the late 1930s. Later, in 1853, a successful analytical engine appeared in Sweden, and one was produced in the United States in 1858.

Business machines and calculators, all mechanical, made their appearance in Europe and the United States toward the end of the nineteenth century, marking the beginning of some of the large manufacturers of today's calculators. Now there are hundreds of firms in the field, spurred on by the development of new minicomputers, microcomputers, and the development of newer and less expensive peripherals.

The development of components such as relays, vacuum tubes, transistors, and integrated circuits facilitated the development of the modern computer and its peripheral hardware. Harvard University, in conjunction with the International Business Machines Corporation (IBM) and the Bell Telephone Laboratories (BTL), developed between 1940 and 1942 a series of relay computers. Although exhibiting a high degree of reliability, they were quickly superseded by much faster all-electronic vacuum tube computers. The relay machine peripherals were limited to switches, lights, and teletype equipment. The first vacuum tube computer was ENIAC, designed by the University of Pennsylvania's Moore School of Engineering and installed at the Aberdeen Proving Ground in 1946 for the purpose of cleaning up the backlog of ballistics calculations that had accumulated during World War II. Although ENIAC was not basically a machine that operated with binary arithmetic, it admirably performed the task it had been designed for. The flip-flop circuit, patented in 1919 and used until then only in radar equipment, was the critical component in the design of ENIAC. Although all-electronic, ENIAC's design was never duplicated, because of the difficulty of assigning to it purely scientific problems. Retired from service in the late 1950s, it contained 33,000 vacuum tubes and occupied an entire room that had to be air-conditioned to keep the tubes cool. Peripheral equipment was the same as for the electromechanical machines, except for the addition of a magnetic drum memory (discussed in Chapter 3).

A host of all-binary machines followed, among which were EDVAC, SEAC, and WHIRLWIND (primarily scientific computers), and the IBM 604. Late in the 1950s commercial machines appeared, including the IBM 704 and the Honeywell 400 and 800 series. With the implementation of integrated circuit production, numerous commercial/scientific computers were marketed with the introduction of the Honeywell 2200 series, the RCA Spectra series, and the IBM 360 series, followed later by the IBM 370 series—all the results of the integrated circuit trend starting in 1967. Peripherals now also included disk files, high-speed tape reader/recorders, printers, plotting equipment, cathode-ray tubes, and interfaces to control such devices as machines, aircraft navigation equipment, and weapon systems (all basically analog devices), that require interfacing devices usually called *converters*, which convert from or to a varying level of voltage variation or shaft rotation to or from a digital format. Devices working on voltage levels or shaft rotation are known as *analog devices*. Basically this conversion problem is easier to solve today, since the peripheral interface converters are much smaller, less expensive, and have a high degree of accuracy. Late in the 1960s the minicomputer made its initial appearance, and about 1972 the microcomputer (originally used for digital watches and hand calculators) made their initial appearances. Presently the microcomputer is replacing the minicomputer for most functions: either is as powerful and much faster than the earlier computers of the 1950s or 1960s. Costs are now quite low, which has also affected the pricing of peripherals, since they should be in a proportionately comparable price range.

1-5 BASIC COMPUTER ORGANIZATION

A diagram of a basic computer organization is shown in Fig. 1-1. Here the arithmetic unit performs all the calculations. Its operations, and in fact all data flow back and forth from both memory (internal) and the input/output (I/O) interfacing block, are under control of the control block which calls both data and instructions from memory under control of machine instructions. The memory, therefore, is the storage place for both the data and the machine instructions. Normally, both machine instructions and data are listed in sequence, stored in sequential cells, and given an address number (location specification). This permits the control to call for an address and to sequence the desired program step by step—or jump to a different starting address—completing a special program segment called a *subroutine*, then jumping back to the original program and continuing from the point following the subroutine jump. The control block thus (1) accepts machine instructions in sequence and decodes them, (2) causes data flow in or out of the arithmetic unit, (3) transfers data in or out of the memory and input/output block as well. Thus, since it also transfers the memory stored commands as well, it is the real commander of the computer. Lastly, there is the input/output block, which provides access to the outside world via the peripheral devices.

Machine instructions are of many types, differing with each com-

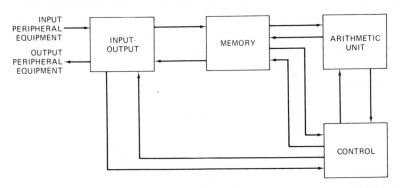

FIGURE 1-1 Basic computer organization.

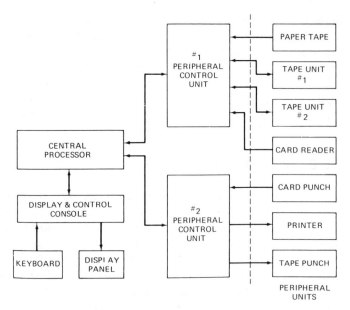

FIGURE 1-2 A sample computer with peripherals.

puter internal registers, automated transfers under peripheral control, control types, but also additional types that transfer data between computer internal registers, automated transfers under peripheral control, instructions that shift numbers within a register, instructions that test the operation of the computer and the peripherals, instructions to modify instructions, instructions that change the number system, and many others which vary with the computer's organization and anticipated operating programs.

All the computer sections mentioned above are built from digital logic, which has changed greatly during the past 25 years. A typical computer system is illustrated by Fig. 1-2. In this case the central processor and control are combined in an arithmetic logic unit (ALU), which incorporates both arithmetic processing and control. The peripheral control units (PCUs) are the input/output interfacing devices. They do their job of tying the high-speed computer to the slower peripherals. This is merely a typical example. Details are left to later chapters.

1-6   LOGIC BLOCKS AND DEFINITIONS

Although the subject of this book is peripherals and their controls, logic elements and blocks will be shown in the diagrams. The reader is referred to a good book on digital logic for details on that subject. Table 1-1 outlines the fundamental operations and devices as well as defining

TABLE 1-1

LOGIC ELEMENTS AND LOGIC BLOCKS

Element	Symbol	Explanation
A. Simple logic elements:		
1. AND gate (or coincident gate)		*If all inputs are true (1), then the output is (1).*
2. OR gate		*If any input is true (1), then the output is true (1).*
3. NAND gate (not-AND)		*If all inputs are true (1), then the output is (0).*
4. NOR gate (not-OR)		*If any input is true (1), then the output is (0). If no input is true, then the output is (1).*
5. Inverter		*Inverts a (1) to a (0) or a (0) to a (1).*

TABLE 1-1 (Continued)

Element	Symbol	Explanation
6. Exclusive-OR		*For two (1) inputs or two (0) inputs the output is (0). If one input is a (1) and the other a (0), the output is a (1).*
7. Exclusive-NOR		*The inversion of the exclusive-OR.*
8. Flip-flops	R/S	*A device that is set or reset. If set the Q output is (1) and the Q output is (0). If reset the outputs Q and Q̄ are reversed.*
	JK	*This is an R-S flip-flop. A J-K flip-flop changes its state only during a clock pulse.*
	D	*A D flip-flop changes its state during the rising edge of the clock pulse.*

9. One-shot multivibrator

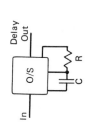

A circuit that generates a delay, depending on the R-C values applied

B. Simple combinational element blocks:

1. Decoder

Depending on input binary code, 1 of n outputs are selected. For 3 inputs 8 outputs are selectable. For 4 inputs 16 outputs are selectable; 5 inputs, 32 outputs; etc.

2. Counter

Several flip-flops are combined in a single package. For example, 4 FFs can count up to 16, or the circuit can be designed to count to 10 or 12—in fact, any number up to 16. 8 FFs can count to 16×16, or 256, etc. 4 FF counters can be connected in series to count up to any number of pulses.

3. Shift register

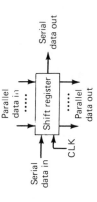

These units can input in parallel, output in parallel, input in series, output in series. For serial operation the binary number shifts in from left to right or right to left; every time it is clocked, it shifts 1-bit position. These devices are employed often to convert a parallel binary number to serial number, or visa versa.

TABLE 1-1 (*Continued*)

Element	Symbol	Explanation
4. Latch		*Up to 8 FFs can be packaged in a single package. These are used to store binary data until their use are desired.*
5. Parallel adder		*This unit will sum or subtract up to 4 binary bit additions. Depending on the design, the output can be the binary sum or difference, or binary coded decimal (BCD). These units can be cascaded.*
6. Parity generator/checker		*This unit will generate even or odd parity depending on the number of (1s) and (0s) in the input word.*
7. Tri-state gates		*This circuit converts a bidirectional bus to an input and output bus. This is normally used to connect microcomputer buses to peripherals having either an input or output bus connection.*

C. Converters

1. Analog/digital (A/D)

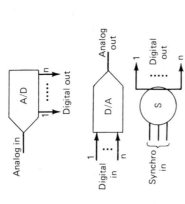

These devices accept analog inputs usually via a multiplexer and output a digital code indicating the signal amplitude. Used primarily for dc signals.

2. Digital/analog (D/A)

The opposite to the above. It accepts up to 16-bit digital codes and converts these to an analog dc voltage level.

3. Synchro/digital

These devices accept the 3-phase ac input from a synchro and code the angle as a digital code.

4. Synchro/sin θ/cos θ

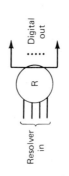

These accept synchro outputs and generate dc output voltages equal to the sin and cosine of the synchro position angle.

5. Resolver converters

Resolvers are four-wire position indicators, and they can generate digital code outputs of the angle also.

them in general terms. Most of the figures will be in block form, where the block title defines its usage.

This table generally defines elements and combinational logic elements. There are many more used in computer diagrams, among them internal memories of several classifications such as addressable random memories (RAMs), which store temporary material in an addressable mode—that is, the control unit provides an address to the memory cells in a random mode—read only memories (ROMs) of which the contents are unchangeable and can be only read, and pROMs, which can be changed by special processes, but are, once set, basically ROMs. Both of these above types can possess one of several logic structures. RAMs may have bipolar logic or a refresh form made up of metal oxide semiconductors (MOS). There are two forms of these (p-MOS and n-MOS), with p-MOS being the faster of the two. Also, coming to the forefront is integrated-integrated logic (I^2L), which has all the properties of bipolar logic (TTL) but is processed as unipolar logic (n-MOS and p-MOS). Another type that should be mentioned is c-MOS, which is a combination of p-MOS and n-MOS but generally employs less power. p-MOS is slower than n-MOS but appeared first after bipolar logic. n-MOS is about ten times faster and approaches TTL in speed. A new logic now used by Texas Instruments is I^2L, which is equivalent to TTL except that each gate element takes less chip area per gate than TTL. Also, new logic such as H-MOS is making its appearance. It is faster than n-MOS and should challenge I^2L in the long run. Several manufacturers, including Motorola, are using it in new designs.

These are by no means all the sensors of analog signals that are converted to digital formats. Such items as shaft encoders, weight sensors, temperature sensors, liquid level sensors are examples of other converters. There is one more device that should be mentioned, the universal asynchronous receiver transmitter (UART). This device is used in digital communication systems to provide conversion back and forth from computer parallel busses to serial data transmission over two-wire telephone or other serial data lines not requiring a MODEM (as discussed in Chapter 7).

1-7 INTERFACING

1-7.1 Minicomputers

The details of the interfacing process are primarily delegated to Chapters 2 and 6, but an introduction is given here. Generally, a minicomputer has three separated buses and several control lines. Most often, a 16-bit input and separate output buses are provided, along with a peripheral address bus, and at least one interrupt line—although there can be more. Generally, the input (or output) buses are active at the same time the address bus is activated, which permits movement of data between the peripheral desired and the processor, with the address bus directing the data flow. Chapter 6 gives additional detail and defines data flow under processor control (DIO) or under peripheral device control (BIO), or more commonly known now as *direct memory access* (DMA). There are, in addition, half a dozen or so control lines and at least one or more interrupt lines. As pointed out in Chapter 6, DIO and BIO will probably have a different set of control lines, in addition to DIO's three sets of buses. Data buses are usually 16-bits wide and parallel, and the address bus usually at least 10-bits wide and also parallel.

1-7.2 Microcomputers

The early microcomputers introduced bidirectional buses. These varied from 4-bits wide to the present 16 or more bits wide. Also, the buses carried both address and data information. If the peripheral address and data are carried on separate buses, the data transfer is generally faster. This can be observed with the bit-chip design covered in Chapter 2 versus the designs using multifunctioned buses. When 4-bit buses were employed for bidirectional data and addressing functions, the transfer time was delayed simply by the fact that both functions were transferred 4 bits at a time in sequence. This disadvantage has been eliminated from many of the newer processors and some even have dual bidirectional buses.

Even the minicomputers have now adopted bidirectional buses, which could be inferred from Chapter 2 since minicomputers are now built from microcomputer parts. For many designs, separate control lines and interrupts are also part of the package.

1-8 MAINTENANCE

The term *maintenance* is hard to define. Some routine maintenance can be performed by the user (such as cleaning recording heads and other routine maintenance as specified by the user manual furnished with each peripheral). Even cards can be replaced if spares are available and on hand. Usually a peripheral is furnished under a manufacturer's guarantee specifying replacement and repair cards for a certain time period. After the period expires a maintenance contract can often be negotiated—for a fee, of course.

Unless the user has a maintenance staff, it probably would be just as well to have the job done elsewhere, but cost considerations may warrant consideration of the staff approach. Other factors could include the length of time required to secure adequate repairs, the ability of the supplier's maintenance staff, and other considerations such as special tools required for adequate and accurate adjustments and equipment needed to prove out maintenance procedures.

1-9 CHOOSING PERIPHERALS

Choice of the most suitable complement of peripherals depends on a system's usage, the type of system, and whether or not it is distributed. In a general system printers, plotters, mass memory, and other monitoring equipment, including data loading or unloading equipment, are near the main processor, but the D/A, A/D converters and other sensing devices are near the distributed processors. Choice is directly influenced by the anticipated reliability and the variety of uses required of the equipment. Some factors affecting choice include:

1. The environment: for example, is the system needed for a military project?
2. The required speed of operation.
3. Will an observer or technician be required?
4. Is the interface common to others in the system?
5. What is the required maintenance? Can it be done by regular personnel, or is factory assistance required and how expensive would that be?
6. What is the total cost for acquisition, including first costs, software, and maintenance, as well as the length of time of useful life and replacement cost?

These are just a few of the things one must consider. Additional factors affecting choice of equipment obviously would depend on special needs or usage.

1-10 SUMMARY

Topics covered in this chapter are definitions and classifications of typical peripherals and a short history—outlining a history of processors and the basics of digital processors from early times to the present. Primary processor examples include the ENIAC and EDVAC of the late 1940s and early 1950s, the minicomputers of the late 1960s and early 1970s, and the microprocessor of the 1970s and 1980s. Both minicomputers and microcomputers are now commonplace, but in many instances the large machines of the 1960s are still being used to their capacity, because their programming and software have been operated for years, and there has been no urgent need to change to newer equipment as they serve specific purposes adequately. Usually, the most costly part of an installation is the programming, unless a standard program can be purchased that has already been proven out—that has been debugged of all errors. The debugging process to get a newly written program into correct form is often very costly.

Although this book covers peripheral devices in detail, there is some coverage of logic blocks and logic generally. Table 1-1 is included for that purpose.

Since one talks about interfacing when discussing and considering an added peripheral, this topic is introduced briefly, along with maintenance and the process of choosing the peripherals to be purchased. The remainder of the book covers these topics in detail, except for maintenance. Usually, the supplier of a peripheral will provide a manual that outlines the maintenance procedures that the user can perform. Choosing a peripheral group depends on the problems and programs a system is designed to handle, with an allowance for anticipated future expansion.

Table 1-1 includes some basic logic symbols, but to keep it general the later chapters group individual gates and other logic devices together into blocks so that the reader will focus on the use of the basic building blocks of a processor or peripheral control unit in the following discussions. If logic were included as a separate topic it would add greatly to the length of this book; therefore, the interested reader is referred to books on digital or computer logic for details.

2

Minicomputers and Microcomputers

2-1 A TYPICAL MINICOMPUTER

2-1.1 General

The Interdata 7/16 is a third-generation minicomputer with much greater power than the first-generation machines of the late 1960s. The first-generation machines rapidly penetrated the control market, but the third generation is as powerful as the IBM 360 generation machine: not only can it be used in a typical control operation, but it is powerful and versatile enough to perform business number crunching operations. It, in fact, responds to the IBM 360 family of commands. Basically, it is a hexidecimal (HD) type of computer. Some of the earlier models, such as those made by the Computer Control Division of Honeywell, included a series of computers that were coded in octal numbers. Note: See the Appendix for differences in number codes.

The architecture of the Interdata 7/16 involves 16 registers of 16 bits each comprised as a stack. These registers may store instructions or numbers or act as index registers, thus providing a flexible organization that is easy to use, and adopted by practically all of the microcomputers that rapidly followed, because of the system's capability to use these registers in any way the programmer desires, such as for program instruction storage, temporary data storage, index registers, stack pointers. The versatility of the programmer determines how each register is used. There are, basically, no restrictions. Transfer to and from a memory position is easy and practical.

The central processing unit (CPU) also stores a program status word (PSW), which keeps track of CPU operation, the 16 general registers mentioned before, signed multiply and divide (option), and a floating-point option (FPO) with eight 32-bit registers and the usual instruction counter, three internal buses, and most of the other usual hardware. Figure 2-1 shows a general system block diagram; Fig. 2-2 blocks out the CPU's organization.

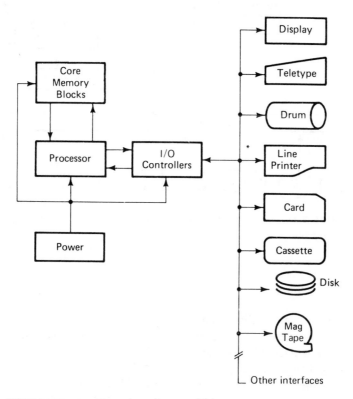

FIGURE 2-1 A typical minicomputer system diagram in block form. (Courtesy Perkin-Elmer Data Systems.)

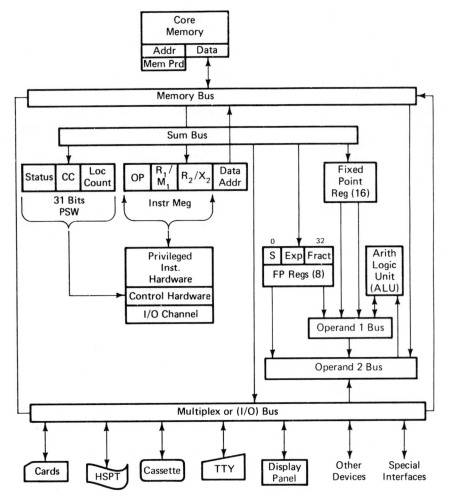

FIGURE 2-2 Interdata processor block diagram. (Courtesy Perkin-Elmer Data Systems.)

2-1.2 Memory

A memory is usually a magnetic core composed of groups of 8K-bytes (KB) that can increment by 8KBs up to 32KBs. The modules are available with a parity bit for accuracy checking. The number of groups is limited by the addressing capability of the bits permitted for instruction addressing codes. One megacycle (1 Mc) is the usual cycle time, but 750 nanosec is available as an option for some models.

2-1.3   Standard Software

Includes:

Symbolic assembler	FORTRAN IV
Basic operating system	BASIC
Interractive text editor	Instructive debug package

2-1.4   Instruction Set

The processor has 90 basic instructions. These use either a 16-bit or 32-bit format. Operations are between registers, between registers and memory, arithmetic, data movement, single-precision floating point (32-bit words), and control. The 64-bit double-precision floating point is not covered, since that is available on only one computer of the line, the Interdata 8/16, which was not available at the time. There is a *16-bit Processor User's Manual* published by Perkin's Elmer Corporation, which provides complete instructions. Generally, instructions provided include logical operations, control operations, arithmetic operations, floating-point operations, and input/output operations. There are instructions for 8-bit bytes, 16-bit words, and 32-bit floating-point words. There are a few instructions which manipulate the program status word (PSW).

2-1.5   Input/Output

There is a dual input/output bus structure that can handle up to 255 devices, including a control panel. High-speed devices via the direct memory access channel (DMA) operate up to 2,000,000 bytes per second, while medium-speed or slow-speed devices can transfer 60,000 bytes per second. Both direct control (DIO) and interrupt automatic vectoring via the interrupt service table are available. DMA was mentioned above, which is available on a byte or full-word basis.

2-1.6   Peripheral Products Available

1. Selector channel
2. Teletype
3. Cathode-ray tube/keyboard
4. Tape cassette
5. Real-time analog system

6. A/D and D/A converters
7. Digital multiplex system
8. Logic interfaces
9. Line printers
10. Card reader/punch
11. Compatible magnetic tapes
12. Disk and floppy disk systems
13. Data set (MODEM) interfaces
14. IBM 360/370 interfaces

2-1.7 Microprogram Control

A macroinstruction addresses the microprogram ROM memory where for each instruction a unique set of microsteps is initiated. As an example, a multiply instruction calls for a series of hexidecimal adds, depending on what the multiplier's value is. On the other hand, a divide instruction requires a series of hexidecimal subtracts. Thus each individual instruction requires a defined set of microsteps in sequence, again depending on the instruction to be executed and the values of the operands themselves.

2-1.8 The Program Status Word (PSW)

The PSW defines the state of the processor at any given time. It is a 32-bit word with the function of individual bits defined in the *16-bit Processor User's Manual* mentioned above. The 11 MSBs indicate the processor's status, while bits 16-32 are the instruction location counter. Bits 12-15, the condition code, are set, according to most instructions, during their execution and are used to signal the instructions function to the remainder of the computer. For example, during a typical instructions execution the condition code bits are set as follows in the tabulation.

Bits:	12	13	14	15	
Code:	C	V	G	L	
	0	0	0	0	Equal comparison or results = 0
	0	0	0	1	Less than
	0	0	1	0	Greater than
	0	1	0	0	Overflow
	1	0	0	0	Carry or borrow

Note: Each instruction will have its own table (see reference quoted).

The LSB bits are the instruction counter and, except for branch instructions, are incremented by "1" during each instructions execution. On branch instructions the counter's contents is replaced by the new address defined by the branch.

2-1.9 Other Compatible Processors of the Interdata Line

Although this chapter treats solely the Interdata 7/16, the other processors of the line are organized in a similar way and include the models 5/16, 6/16, and 8/16. All use the IBM computer models 360/370 instruction formats. The model 5/16 is a small one-board computer having a 600 n-MOS, 600 nanosec memory. Model 6/16 is similar to the 7/16 but has an n-MOS memory in place of a core. The model 8/16 is a core machine but offers several double-precision floating-point instructions. There is a model 7/32, which is a complete 32-bit machine, and consequently its general registers are 32-bits long. In addition, it has an expanded RX format containing up to 47 bits. This allows an absolute address up to 24 bits and 32 bits into the RR format. Also, there are two additional index registers of 32-bit formats. These machines are typical of the latest minicomputers and are powerful enough to perform the most detailed business calculations—hardly possible with first-generation minicomputers, which were restricted to control operations.

2-1.10 The Hexadecimal (HD) Display Panel

This panel provides a means of controlling the processor so as to integrate the various machine states (such as PSW), the program steps, the contents of registers or memory locations, and it can be programmed to act as an I/O device displaying words or bytes. It is equipped with both binary and hexadecimal readouts, as illustrated by Fig. 2-3. Means are provided to enter HD data, addresses, and commands. Among other features are *control keys* that read the entering program (RD), enter address (ADD), enter data or commands by clearing the switch register (DTA), single step the program (SGL), interpret special functions (FN), examine general registers (REG), examine FP registers (FLT), as well as an off/on key, a key to write in memory, and a run key (RUN). The *16-bit Processor User's Manual* contains details on how these keys function and should be consulted for further explanation. Figure 2-4 is another illustration of the control panel.

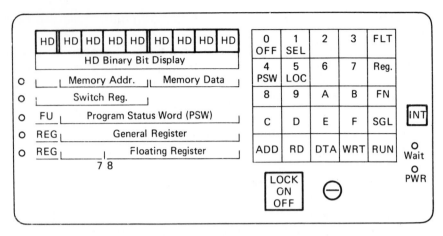

FIGURE 2-3 Hexadecimal display panel.

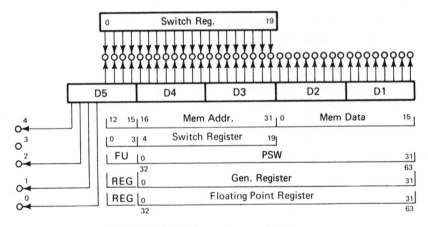

FIGURE 2-4 Display registers and indicators.

2-1.11 Instruction Formats and Details

There are four basic instruction formats employed for normal operation of the computer (see Fig. 2-5). OP represents the operation code; R1 the first operand register; R2 the second operand register; N an intermediate value, which can be plus or minus (used only in the SF class of instructions); X2 is the second operand index register; A is a second operand address; and B is second operand immediate data. The four basic formats are distinguished as register-to-register (RR), short format (SF), register and indexed storage (RX), and register and immediate storage (RI). RR and SF are 16-bit instructions, while RX and RI are 32-bits long.

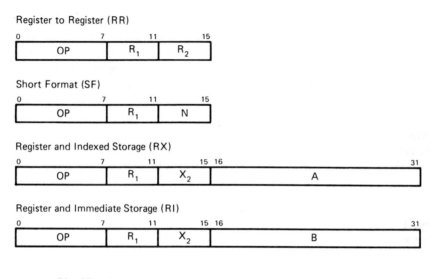

Register to Register (RR)

Short Format (SF)

Register and Indexed Storage (RX)

Register and Immediate Storage (RI)

OP   OP code
R_1 First operand register
R_2 Second operand register
N   A 4-bit immediate value
X_2 Second operand index register
A   Second operand address
B   Second immediate data

FIGURE 2-5   Instruction formats.

2-1.12   Format Details

The details of the formats as explained in Section 2-1.11 are illustrated in Fig. 2-5. The classes of the various instructions are covered in Section 2-1.13.

2-1.13   Classes of Instructions

First of all, there are instructions for the loading and unloading class. These will load and store both commands and data. Following this are the manipulating class, which will move data left or right or rotate registers on themselves for a specified number of HD characters. Other data manipulating instructions are logical operations such as AND, OR, EXCLUSIVE-OR.

These are followed by the arithmetic instructions of the ADD, SUBTRACT, MULTIPLY, COMPARE, and DIVIDE classifications. There is also a set of instructions for examining and changing the PSW word. Another class is that dealing with input/output. And, finally, there is the class dealing with floating-point operations. In the model

8/16 only, there is another class involving 64-bit words, called *precision floating point*. In all models there are the branching instructions which permit the program to jump to a new set of instructions, depending on the results of a program test. These are extremely versatile instructions which permit the program to determine its own course.

In any case, the RR, SF, RX, and RI formats are used repeatedly. The shorter RR and SF formats deal primarily with register operations, while the longer RX and RI usually involve transfers to or from memory, but there are many special cases, such as multiple-word transfers, that require use of 32-bit instructions. Complete details are given in the Interdata manual previously mentioned.

2-2 MICROCOMPUTERS

2-2.1 The Microcomputer Revolution

A microprocessor is an arithmic logic unit (ALU) having the necessary adder, accumulator, program counter, stack registers, pointer, control logic, and buses. Generally, to convert a microprocessor (μ-processor or μP) into a microcomputer one must add read-only memory (ROM) and random access memory (RAM), although a limited amount is sometimes included on an ALU chip. In most cases, however, additional ROM and RAM are required and added as additional chips. The stack register is very much like that of the Interdata 7/16, having a stack pointer to address words in a register stack. Although originally the need in calculators and digital watches was for 4-bit BCD words, control applications were demanding 8-bit and 16-bit designs. These were developed in 1972, but in fact, it is sometimes difficult to decide whether a minicomputer or microcomputer is necessary to solve a particular problem or to control a process.

Although control personnel originally adopted 4-bit designs, these units were soon superseded by 8-bit and 16-bit units. In fact, Motorola and National make the equivalent of a 32-bit minicomputer. Since most control operations use ASC II code, 8-bit designs quickly followed with the Intel model 8008 (a redesigned 4004), the Motorola M6800, and a new Intel 8080A. Sixteen-bit designs originally grouped together four 4-bit chips, or two 8-bit chips, but eventually Texas Instruments developed its 990 series, which features several 16-bit designs with a single ALU, and this has also included the microNOVA by Data General, the 8086 by Intel, and the Z8000 by Zilog. Also, Motorola has several improved versions of the M6800 and a new 16-bit/32-bit MC68000. Because of the added power additional applications have evolved, and since the newer minicomputers use microprocessor components the distinction between them is rapidly fading. The first microprocessors were p-MOS circuit designs, but n-MOS brought about a 10-fold speed increase, and I^2L and H-MOS are very much faster. Originally, microcomputers were used in applications where use of a minicomputer would be an overkill, but all of this is changing rapidly. It is almost impossible to keep abreast of developments. An example would be to use a minicomputer to control a single traffic light. It makes more sense to put a microprocessor at the light and to evaluate the individual microprocessors with a minicomputer or a more elaborate microcomputer.

2-2.2 Microprocessor Stacks

Typical microprocessors employ stack registers. These are recent additions in the minicomputer field with third-generation designs. A stack is simply a sequential ordering of registers. A word may be entered into the register where the pointer indicates. Thus, a word is pushed onto the stack, and a word below is pushed down one position. Words above are left undisturbed. To remove words from the stack a pop operation is performed (the reverse of the push operation), and the word at the pointer is removed. This form of stack is known as *last-in-first-out* (LIFO) to describe its push-pop method of operation.

One other point concerns register addressing via the pointer. If the stack contains eight words, a 3-bit pointer would be sufficient. In many early microprocessors the stack held a list of sequential instructions. By changing the pointer address, words were moved upward or downward in the stack. Normally, a stack is charged with a great many data words or instructions. When considering the execution of instructions, the command is popped out into the MAR and command decoder matrix.

Stack architecture eases the problems of skips and jumps. If, for example, a jump is received, a starting address for the interrupt servicing is pushed onto the stack, and the program counter's (P-C) new address proceeds from there. The program address before receiving the interrupt is pushed downward, and when the interrupt has finished being serviced, the original program is restored and its operation continues. Depending on the microprocessor's design, stacks can be in internal registers or arranged in order as memory positions. Both designs are popular. In any case, the P-C is incremented by "1" and, because the interrupt program is pushed onto the stack, at its completion the beginning of the original program is in position for the pointer to continue to exercise it.

Hardware stacks are limited in length, but access is generally faster. Memory stacks can be much longer, but it takes more time to access

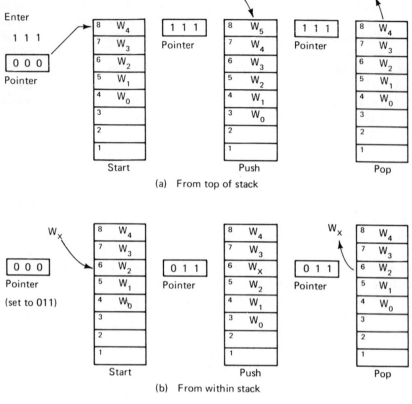

FIGURE 2-6 Push and pop operations for stacks.

them. After a subroutine has been completed, it is popped off the stack. Figure 2-6 illustrates the operation of a stack.

2-2.3 A Typical Microcomputer

Figure 2-7 blocks out a typical microcomputer. The microprocessor itself provides (1) machine control function, (2) the program counter, (3) the instruction register, (4) the address stack, (5) the arithmetic unit (ALU), and (6) the accumulator. Some processors have separate external buses for data and command movements between RAM, ROM, and I/O. In addition, there will be the control lines and possibly also interrupts. In the simple system outlined in Fig. 2-7 all transfers are via the system bus. In this case commands, data transfers, etc., must be multiplexed in turn—thus, a decided speed improvement is available in multibus systems, especially where commands and data do not share and thus congest the single bus.

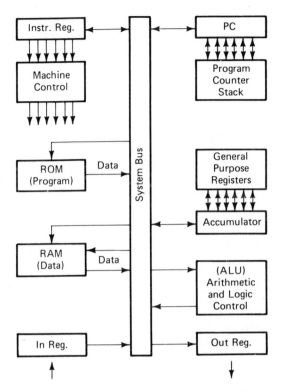

FIGURE 2-7 Generalized microprocessors block diagrams. Basic machine cycle-PC addresses next command code to ROM. ROM code is sent to instruction register (IR). Control decodes IR and directs instruction execution. If memory reference instruction, RAM will be addressed. RAM will send or receive data from accumulator. If so instructed, ALU will alter data. These six steps are the sequence for a microprocessor.

2-2.4 Microcomputer Features

Microprocessors are distinguished by their use of LSI technology. This approach has been extended to ROMs, RAMs, and even specialized interface chips. Some of the more common attributes are instruction sets that are compatible with minicomputers; both direct and indirect addressing as well as indexing may be provided. Usually, stack addressing software and instructions are included. Software availability is now about equivalent to that available for minicomputers. Interrupt capability is important and generally extensive on the newer machines. Execution time is generally longer for p-MOS and n-MOS machines than for TTL, but the newer technologies I^2L and H-MOS are closing the time gap. Interfacing should be compatible to TTL levels. Now special MSIs and LSIs are provided. Memory, both RAM and ROM, is usually not part of the ALU chip, but there are exceptions. Quite often timing clocks and power supplies must be externally applied. In some cases small ROMs and RAMs are a part of the microprocessor ALU chip, but usually, like the 8080A and M6800, these memories are external groups of chips.

2-2.5   Intel 8080A

One of the most popular microprocessors since 1975 has been the Intel 8080 (now 8080A), as shown diagramatically in Fig. 2-8. The ALU handles 8-bit quantities via its adder and accumulator. Its stack registers are internal and composed of three 16-bit registers. Because the ALU accumulator is only 8-bits wide, the three general 16-bit registers are treated as if they were six 8-bit registers. The processor generally operates on 8-bit bytes. All this data flow is over bidirectional 8-bit paths. Data and instructions enter the ALU on an 8-bit bus,

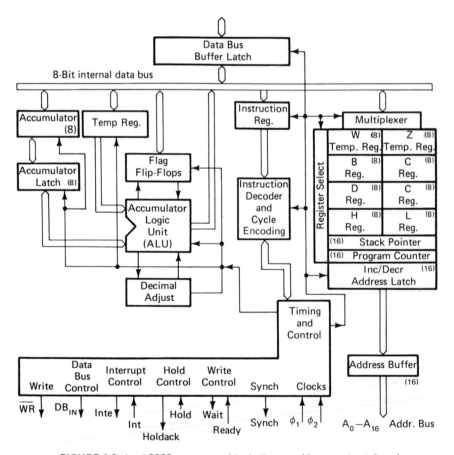

FIGURE 2-8   Intel 8080 μ-processor block diagram. (Courtesy Intel Corp.)

where instructions are sent to the instruction register and then decoded for control. The processor controls data flow along internal bus paths. I/O data flows via the accumulator and the I/O buffer. Two 16-bit counting registers are on the chip (1) for program location and (2) as a push-pop stack counter-controller. The P-C sends out a 16-bit address on the address bus to address memory modules and fetch and process instructions. The P-C is incremented by "1" each time it is used. The 8080A had 78 instructions according to a recent count.

The processor organization and its functions are outlined below.

1. Register array and address logic: A static RAM is provided to form either three 16-bit registers or six 8-bit registers. This permits an unlimited facility for subroutine nesting. Also provided is a 16-bit program counter (P-C), which essentially contains the present memory address, and a stack pointer, which addresses the next stack location in memory. Finally, register pairs B-C, D-E, and H-L are three 16-bit registers or six 8-bit registers, employed to hold data or addresses, etc. These registers are program addressable. Temporary register pairs W-Z are used for internal instructions and are not addressable. Except for registers W-Z, 16-bit addresses from any of the other registers can be incremented and put in the address latch for addressing memory.

2. Arithmetic logic unit (ALU): The ALU performs arithmetical, logical, and rotational features. The components functioning within the ALU include the following:
   (a) 8-bit accumulator
   (b) 8-bit temporary accumulator
   (c) 8-bit temporary register
   (d) 5-bit sign register

   Decimal arithmetic is performed directly by a DAA instruction using auxiliary carries.

3. Instruction register (I-R) and control section: The I-R and the timing and control provide instruction op-code decoding. Inputs are from the Ø1 and Ø2 clocks, the ready, interrupt, reset, hold control signals, as well as the INTE, NLDA, DB, SYNC, WR, and WAIT strobes.

4. Data bus buffer: The data bus is bidirectional and is buffered from the internal processor logic by the data bus buffer. This approach allows many devices and memory elements to interface with the processor without loading down the internal logic.

   The instruction cycle performs in sequence the following steps, but no single instruction will contain more than five steps.
   1. Fetch
   2. Read memory

3. Write in memory
4. Read stack
5. Write stack
6. Input
7. Output
8. Interrupt
9. Halt

2-2.6 Motorola Model M6800

This is the microprocessor unit (MPU) that is in control of the entire microcomputer system. In block diagram form the MPU is shown in Fig. 2-9, with the individual blocks performing the following functions. The output buffer addresses the RAM and any output devices via PLAs or other interfacing chips. The buffer is comprised of

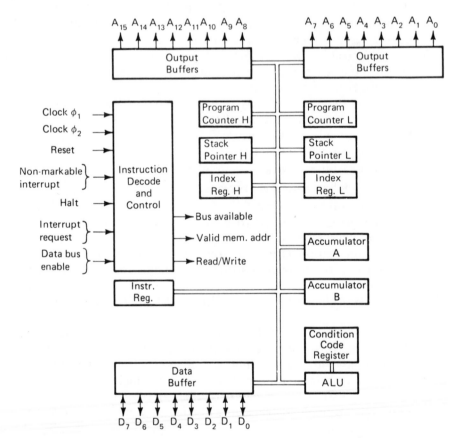

FIGURE 2-9 Motorola M6800 μ-processor block diagram. (Courtesy Motorola Semiconductor Products, Inc.)

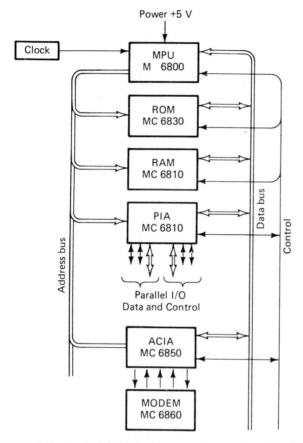

FIGURE 2-10 Motorola M6800 μ-processor and supporting LSIs. (Courtesy Motorola Semiconductor Products, Inc.)

two 8-bit sets, or a total of 16 bits of addressing capability. On these buffers the processor impresses the instruction register, the program counter (H or L), the stack registers (H or L), or the index register (if called for during the instruction execution) and adds to the program counter or instruction register via the ALU. Thus, the summation may be used to address memory during an indexing operation. The bidirectional data interface is furnished by the data buffer. The accumulators are included as two 8-bit units, A and B. The condition code register generally handles carry-out sums or borrows during addition and subtraction processes. An interrupt mask associated with this register controls the recognition of interrupt signals. The interrupt and restart logic, the timing clocks Ø1 and Ø2, the bus control and halt signals, the instruction decoder, and other control signals are all interfaced with the instruction decode and control logic block.

The M6800 microprocessor ALU was the first one to have associated interface chips as a complete family. These included RAM, ROM memories and several interfacing chips. This approach was quickly followed by Intel, RCA, and all other manufacturers. Distinguishing features include complete TTL compatability and a single power supply. There were three sets of bus lines that connected all building blocks which included: (1) a 16-bit address bus, (2) dual 8-bit bidirectional data buses, and (3) ten control lines, including a dual clock, Ø1 and Ø2. An important concept was the tieing together of RAM, ROM memories, and all device interfaces via this standard system. Figure 2-10 summarizes the system architecture. The two interface blocks included, in addition to the ROM and RAM, function as follows:

PIA (parallel interface adapter): This is a dual parallel interface device and permits bidirectional data flow to the addressed device.

ACIA (asynchronous communication interface adapter): This device furnishes a serial interface to such devices as teletypes or MODEMS.

2-2.7 Sixteen-bit Microprocessors

General. Although Fig. 2-11 shows the original concept of paralleling two 8-bit processors to make a 16-bit microprocessor, there are now several 16-bit machines. The earliest was probably the General Data microNOVA, but soon to follow was the Texas Instruments 990 line, which can be purchased for military applications. Early designs, including one by National Semiconductor, paralleled two 8-bit processors. For the approach outlined in Fig. 2-11, 16-bit words are interfaced with memory via two 8-bit buses. Control is via the I-R, μROM, and array matrix. The pointer selects one of several words from the

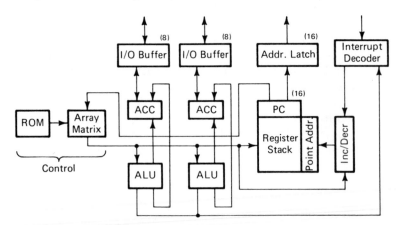

FIGURE 2-11 Sixteen-bit μ-processor block diagram. Although this diagram shows effectively two 8-bit processors in parallel, it is now the practice to make 1-chip μ-processors like the microNOVA or the Texas Instrument TM9900. This is a minicomputer when RAM and I/O interfaces are added.

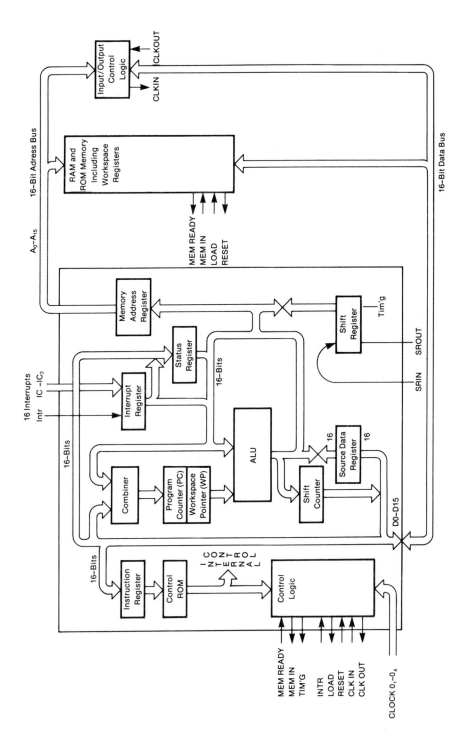

FIGURE 2-12 Sixteen-bit micro/minicomputer.

33

TABLE 2-1

MICROPROCESSOR CHARACTERISTICS

Manufacturer	Intel	Motorola	National Semiconductor	Data General	Texas Instruments
Model	8080A	M6800	N-EO/MP	microNOVA	SBP9900
Material	n-MOS	n-MOS	n-MOS	n-MOS	I^2L
Data bits	8	8	8	16/32	16
Memory bus	16	16	16	16	16
Instructions	116	72	46	—	69
Packaging pins	40	40	40	40	64
Interrupts	1 line	2 lines	—	16	16
				Priority	Priority
Add time	2 μsec	2 μsec	—	—	4 μsec
Memory cycle	700 nanosec	700 nanosec	—	—	280 nanosec

address stack. The instruction register supplies op codes to the array matrix, which selects microcommands from the μROM, providing overall control to the entire system, including the interrupt decoder. All MSI and LSI chips will fit on one or at the most a few cards—a tremendous weight and size advantage over the Interdata 7/16.

A 16-bit Minicomputer Using Microprocessor Components. Several manufacturers now supply 16-bit microprocessors. These are built from p-MOS, n-MOS, I^2L, and H-MOS logic chips. A typical organizational architecture is provided by Fig. 2-12. The program counter (P-C), word pointer (W-P), ALU, and status register comprise the ALU, but in the organization shown the stack registers are not. These have been moved to external memory, and these areas, consisting of several words, are designated as work space, and 16 words are designated by the W-P as if they were internal hardware registers. Thus, 16 words of memory become the internal registers that we find in the Interdata 7/16 or Intel 8080A. This is more like the M6800, is it not? A change in the contents of the P-C will designate another work space area. To restore the original program work space, register 13 will store the original W-P, register 14 the original P-C, and register 15 the original status word. Register O stores the number of bits a word is to be shifted. Otherwise, 12 registers can store commands, data, calculation results, temporary data, etc.

Thus, memory has two functions: (1) regular memory and (2) work space and can be programmed in any combination for these two functions.

The source data registers temporarily store parallel input or output words. The MAR has its usual function. Data can also be input or output via a shift register by employing a SRIN or SROUT. The shift counter controls the number of bits shifted for each byte or word. The memory can be a combination of ROM and RAM, where the RAM is programmed to be either normal memory or work spaces. Table 2-1 lists the characteristics of several microprocessors.

TABLE 2-2

TSM9901	*Programmable system interface*
TMS9902	*Asynchronous communication controller*
TMS9903	*Synchronous communication controller*
TMS9904	*Clock generator*
TMS9905	*Single bus inputs*
TMS9906	*Latch outputs*
TMS9907	*Interrupt inputs*
TMS4042	*256 × 4 static ROM*
TMS4043	*256 × 4 static RAM*
TMS4051	*Static RAM refresh for cycle stealing*
TMS9911	*UART serial interface*

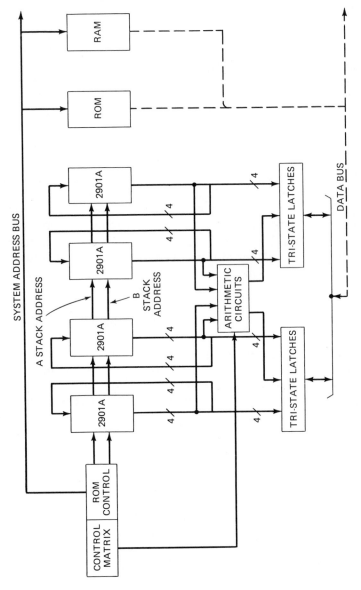

FIGURE 2-13 A block diagram of a bit-slice processor.

Input or output can be provided to a number of devices. Eight-
or 16-bit parallel and serial input/outputs are available. Special I/O
cards can be purchased which have a number of unique possibilities.
Table 2-2 provides an example of special devices available for the Texas
Instruments 990 series, including the TMS9900 or SBP9900.

A Bit-slice Microprocessor. Bit-slice processors are often built
from 2901A or 2903A chips and associated chips, as illustrated in the
diagram of Fig. 2-13. Each of these chips has an internal 16 X 4 register. Four of these chips can be combined to provide a fast 16-bit
processor. There are two separate stack address buses, A and B. These
can be used separately or, in fact, at the same time to add or delete
words from the stack register. In addition, there are several strobes
required and up to 16-priority interrupts. The 48-pin 2903A is like the
40-pin 2901A, except that it has additional add, subtract, multiply, and
divide capabilities. These and the associated chips are available from a
number of suppliers, including National Semiconductor, Advanced
Micro Devices, Harris, Signetics and others. The clock rate can be up to
8 MHz, and speed is obtained by employing separate data and address
buses. Input/output buses are tri-state, bidirectional, with suitable buffer registers for driving output lines and storing input data. Additional
chips are readily available, and a complete processor requires less than
20 chips, except for ROM and RAM memories.

2-3 EXAMPLES OF MICROCOMPUTER APPLICATIONS

1. Process control equipment for data gathering and reduction.
2. Intelligence control for trains, autos, and assembly lines.
3. Intelligence control and navigation for aircraft.
4. Medical equipment for radiation measurement of laboratory gear.
5. Measurement systems—sensor control of flow process monitoring or heat control.
6. Educational systems—for example, microfilm reading/record-
   ing and automatic library searches.
7. Automated pollution control, automobile ignition and
   diagnostic systems.
8. Multiprocessing engineering systems.
9. Industrial appliances and utility control.
10. Multiplexers, MODEMs, and communication control.

11. Intelligence terminals, including display unit records. One such example is an airline reservation system.

12. Small business computers of many varieties.

13. Special-purpose terminals that read badges or items being checked out at a supermarket.

14. I/O channels for large computers.

15. Automatic typesetting for newspapers.

16. Stand-alone desk-top computers.

17. Banking terminals and cash dispensers.

18. Automatic time clocks and payroll systems.

19. Building controllers such as elevators, security systems, and environmental control.

20. Manufacturing control systems such as testers, analyzers, etc.

2-4   A BUSINESS MINICOMPUTER

This computer is a powerful desk-top computer that is ideal for many scientific, engineering, and business applications involving data acquisition, control, or both, as well as business management. The system includes 56K bytes of memory expandable to 449K bytes, CRT with a graphics option (an optional built-in thermal line printer). This system, provided by Hewlett-Packard (HP), is their capable model 9845B. HP's language-extended BASIC is recommended as a programming language. The system also includes dual tape drives, with the second one optional. Also optional are cassette drives, disks of various types, and other peripherals.

The enhanced BASIC language is easy to use but much more powerful than normal BASIC. It has many of the features of FORTRAN or ATL and provides for unified mass storage operations regardless of the storage chosen. The user employs the same set of statements, whether the storage is a flexible disk, cassette, or a cartridge that can store up to 217K bytes. Language consistency saves time and reprogramming when addressing different storage devices.

The interface capability is also extensive. It features chip interfaces for standard devices and parallel interfaces that include 6-bit BCD, ASC II, IEEE-Std.-488 (1978), DIO, BIO (DMA), and 15 levels of programmable priority interrupt. Other interfacing provided includes a serial RS232C bus.

The CRT is an integral part of the desk-top computer. The tube face measures 12 in. diagonally, and in its alphanumeric mode contains 24 lines of 80 characters for viewing data, list programs, display key-

TABLE 3-3

CHARACTERISTICS OF PAPER TAPE DEVICES

Manufacturer	Superior Electric	Facit	Facit	Facit	Decitek
Model	Slo-syn	4070	4040	4020	243
Tracks	Up to 8	Up to 8	Up to 8	Up to 8	Up to 8
Chars./sec	200	75	Can punch and read	300	600
Ft of tape	750	750	650	750	500
Reel size	8"	8"	8"	8"	7.5"
Reader	*		120	*	
Punch		*	75		*
Read method	LEDS/Photocells	None	Optical	Optical	Fiber optics
Dimensions	8.8H×19W×10D"	10.5H×19W×7.8D"	9H×19W×16D"	5.3D×19W×18D"	8.7H×19W×6.8D"
Weight	35 lb	30 lb	10 lb	28.6 lb	21 lb
Power	—	200 W	—	120 W av.	230 W
Notes:	This firm also makes a 300 char./sec unit		Two devices in one		This firm makes readers down to 150 chars./sec

Note: All of these models can increase tape length by a substitution of thinner tape. Most models will read a punch translucent Mylar tape as well as paper tape.

*The asterisks point to whether the device is a punch or reader. The Facit Model 4040 will perform both punching and reading. It is the only dual device tabulated.

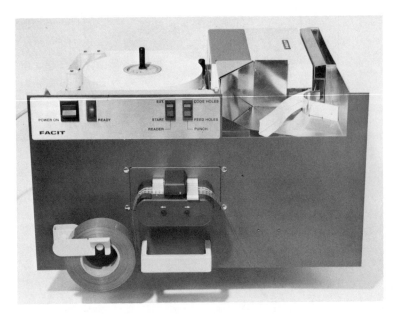

FIGURE 3-2 Tape punch/reader combination. (Courtesy Facit Data Product Div, Facit Inc.)

comprised both a reader and a punch operating at the standard Teletype speed of 10 characters per second. Interfacing units were necessary to change codes between the Teletype equipment and any printers, tape readers/punches, and the RS232 interface to or from the Teletype equipment line terminal.

As previously mentioned, present high-speed tape readers are generally photoelectric devices that use a common light source and individual photocell detectors for each track.

For the paper tape punch, there is an interposer placed between the cam and punch pin for the individual track punches. When the interposer is left in a neutral position, no hole is punched. When it is positioned, the punch pin passes through the paper to create a hole. The number of tracks can be anywhere from five to nine, depending on the code employed. If a parity bit is used, the minimum Baudot code character would take 6 bits. For ASC II and a parity bit there would be eight tracks. The EBCDIC code discussed in Appendix A-6.2 can accommodate 9 bits with parity. Parity is explained in Chapter 6.

3-2 CARD DEVICES

Hollerith (IBM) cards also serve as loading and unloading devices. When so used the cards are loaded via an input hopper and collected after use in an output hopper. They are routed through the reading or punching position one card at a time, traveling in the direction parallel to their long side. On a typical card, 80 characters can be stored by the 80 columns. Other storage forms are possible, but the character method is the most common. The code employed is shown in Fig. 3-3 and is called the *Hollerith code*. Note that it differs in form from the ASC II code; a translation process is often required within the processor to make card-stored and tape-stored data compatible. Card punches can process up to 300 cards per minute, and reading rates can exceed 1200 cards per minute. Card equipment punches holes mechanically (as for paper tape) and reads either mechanically, photoelectrically, or electrically by wire brushes in the same manner as for paper tape. Characteristics of card devices are listed in Table 3-4.

Hollerith cards can be punched mechanically by a key punch or automatically by an automatic card punch. The key punch is basically composed of two hoppers; the cards are transferred individually from the right-hand hopper to the manual punch position, where the operator manually punches in characters in successive positions from left to right. After the last column is punched the board passes to the bottom position in the left-hand hopper, where it is temporarily stored. In addition to character keys, the operator has access to several control keys on the keyboard. These extra keys permit the operator to control the operation of the key punch, such as rejecting a card because of a mistake or having to move a bunch of cards from the right-hand hopper to the output, or left-hand hopper. This process continues for all cards in the input hopper (usually, about 500). As cards are punched the right-hand stack depletes, and the left-hand stack builds up.

To input cards to the computer an automatic card reader is employed. The finished stack is loaded into a loading hopper, and the cards are read from left to right, one column at a time, in sequence, starting with the bottom card, through the read mechanism, and to the lowest card position of the left-hand hopper. As the right-hand stack depletes, the left-hand stack builds up.

In some cases an automatic card punch is used to punch an output deck, reflecting the results of the computer processing. Automatic

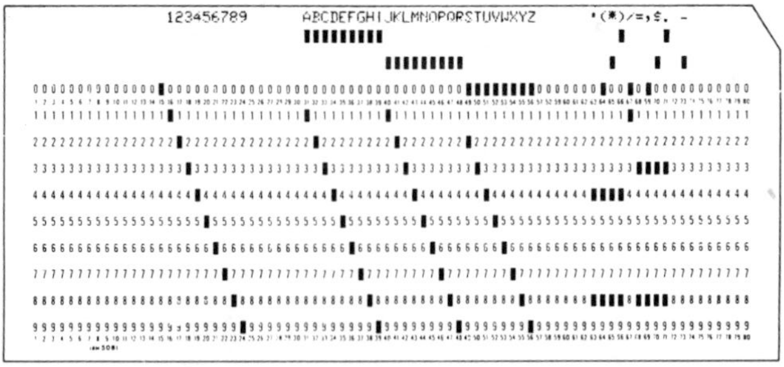

FIGURE 3-3 Hollerith code on a typical punched card.

TABLE 3-4

CHARACTERISTICS OF CARD DEVICES

Manufacturer	Burroughs		Perkins-Elmer	Mohawk Data Sciences	
Model	122	B303	—	EF-4C-CON	ERD
Punch	—	100 cpm sidewise	—	210 cpm	
Reader	200 cpm		400-1000 cpm		1000 cpm
Hopper size (cards)	500	500	500-1000	1000	1000
Data lines	12	80	12	12	12
Reading method	Photocell	—	Photocell		Optical
Codes	Hollerith binary	Hollerith binary	Hollerith	Hollerith	Hollerith
Weight	300 lb	1200 lb	—	500 lb	250 lb
Dimensions	42W×30H×19D"	53.5H×44.5W×28D"		35W×60H×35D" table mount	35W×35H×32D" table mount
Power	350 W	275 W		2750 W.	1500 W.
Notes			Can make a Hollerith to ASC II conversion	Also 7 control lines	Also 13 control indicators

readers and punches operate at speeds of several hundreds of cards per minute. Since programs can readily be corrected by removing incorrectly punched cards and inserting corrected ones, key punches and other types of card equipment are still widely used. Originally, cards were a form of bulk storage, but this form of memory (because of its bulk) is not included in the discussion of bulk store in Chapter 4, since newer devices are used for most bulk-store applications.

Paper cards are much the same as paper tape, except for the difference in codes employed. Slow readers can make contact through a card hole to the backplate, signifying a hole, by closing a circuit by conduction to the backplate. It is now usual in high-speed readers to use lights and photocell pickups just as for paper tape. The ASC II or EBDIC codes are used normally for paper tape; the Hollerith code is used normally for paper cards. This means that three holes per column are read at one time, but there are exceptions, such as cards holding data in binary code.

Card punches work in a manner similar to paper tape punches, using an interposer to punch holes. The interposers can be set to punch Hollerith code, binary code, or others. Paper tape punches are listed in Table 3-3; specifications for card readers and punches are shown in brief form in Table 3-4.

3-3 MAGNETIC DEVICES

3-3.1 Magnetic Recording and Readback Methods

Audio Recording and Playback. Tape recording was invented in 1896 by Valdemar Poulsen, a Danish physicist. Since then the technology has come a long way, first in audio recordings and later in the recording of digital data. The recording medium is a magnetic tape disk or a paper tape coated with a magnetic material suitable for setting up flux fields generated by passing an electric current through a coil surrounding a soft iron core. There is a gap in the structure adjacent to or touching the recording medium. Magnetic current in the coil causes the flux to jump into the recording medium at the gap.

On playback, the reverse process takes place. Magnets recorded on the tape produces magnetic fluxes across the gap, and these rapidly changing fluxes induce changing fluxes in the core to produce an induced current in the core. That current is sensed by the electronics of the readback amplifier and thus reproduces the original recorded signal.

A simple audio record/readback amplifier is shown schematically in Fig. 3-4.

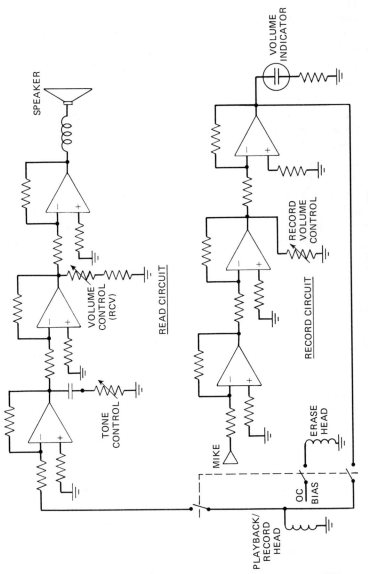

FIGURE 3-4 Audio record/readback amplifier.

An operational amplifier having six amplifiers per I-C package, plus a few other components, can be employed for the total circuit, with three amplifiers in both the record and readback legs. The total gain of either circuit can be controlled by changing the values of the resistors in any of the circuits, but care must be taken so that none of the stages saturate and thus become nonlinear; otherwise recording will be suppressed and readback will be distorted as a consequence. Preceding the record head in the tape path is an erase head which obliterates any previous recording before recording new information. The erase head is normally biased to a saturating current, although a high-frequency alternating current is sometimes employed. On the readback portion both a volume and tone control network are shown. On the record portion an additional gain control is shown, and a resistor/capacitance network provides increase gain at the higher frequencies to counteract the increased noise levels occurring at the high end of the audio spectrum. Most cassette-type audio recorders deteriorate in their frequency response above 5 kHz.

Digital Recording and Readback. Digital recording differs from audio recording methods in that only "1s" and "0s" are stored in the medium. Thus, linear methods are discarded and saturated recording is provided. Various recording codes have existed since 1950. The earliest probably was Miller code, where a "1" saturated the tape (recording medium) in one direction and a "0" in the opposite direction. Readback sensed where the change in flux level to the opposite polarity occurred. An example of this type of recording/readback appears in Fig. 3-5. The major problem with this method was to synchronize the data readback with the remainder of the system timing.

This type of data recording was soon superseded by a form of phase recording. The earliest method was used by the drum memory of the EDVAC computer and recorded by saturating the recording medium with a narrow positive pulse for a "1" and a negative pulse for a "0". A 1 MHz recording was obtained by this method for serial bit stream of "1s" and "0s". Figure 3-6 represents this form of recording and readback.

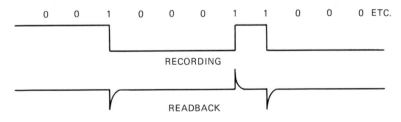

FIGURE 3-5 Miller method of data representation.

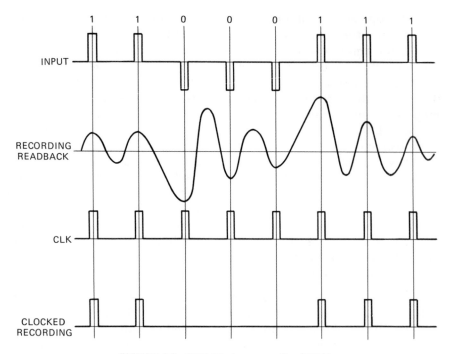

FIGURE 3-6 EDVAC phase recording (1950).

A further improvement was developed in England, called *Manchester*, or *Ferranti, code*. Here a "1" is represented by a flux change from positive to negative pulse in the middle of the bit time interval, and a "0" by a negative to positive change in the middle of the bit time interval. To generate and recover the binary levels the data and clock at the recording end are fed to an exclusive-NOR gate, and thus, Manchester code is generated. For binary data recovery the reverse process occurs. The Manchester code and clock (recovered directly from the code) is again fed to an exclusive-NOR gate, and the binary code reappears in "1", "0" form. The Manchester code not only is still used for digital recording but is the standard for many military and commercial data links. Bell Telephone system and others have their own separate codes. Figure 3-7 outlines Manchester phase recording.

The EDVAC method is termed *return-to-zero* (RZ) recording, but it is a saturated recording, since new data recorded directly over the old data erases the old data. Both Miller and Manchester codes are recorded at saturated levels so both are self-erasing of old data. These are both termed *nonreturn-to-zero* (NRZ) codes.

A data recovery circuit is shown in Fig. 3-8. The first two stages are linear amplifiers. The last stage in line outputs saturated Manchester code. At the output of the second stage the sine wave is fed to two peak detectors, one sensing the positive sine wave peak and the lower one the negative peak. These are combined in separate AND gates with the Manchester output. The two multivibrators provide clocks of the correct width and timing to apply to the exclusive-NOR gate, which in turn provides standard "1" and "0" level binary outputs.

A second method for generating and recovering Manchester code is via four phase-lock loop circuits, which are basically electronic servos. To generate two separate frequencies, two loop circuits generate a separate frequency shift of basic frequency for a "1", and the second a shift in frequency for a "0". A third loop circuit is required to recover and synch the clock for data recovery, which is done by a fourth loop circuit employed as a frequency-shift (FSK) detector. A diagram for this method is shown in Fig. 3-9.

A phase-lock loop system is an electronic servo. A simple method to describe a phase-lock loop (PLL) is to view the input signal as phase compared to the output signal. Thus, input and output frequencies are compared and locked to the input frequency via the path around the

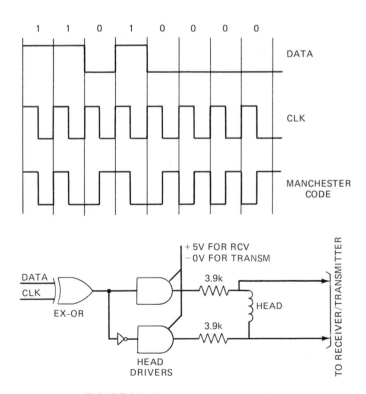

FIGURE 3-7 Manchester phase recording.

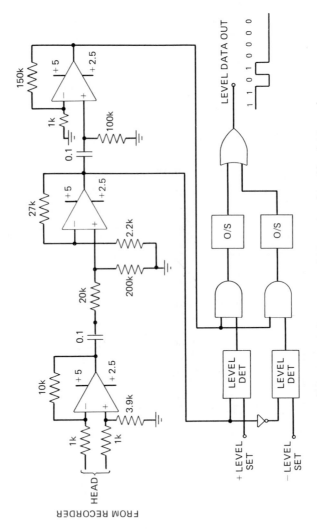

FIGURE 3-8 A circuit for recovery of binary data from Manchester code.

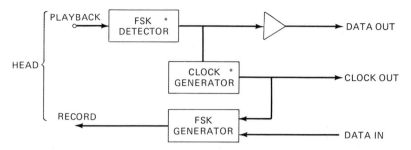

*The same PLL. Note two separate PLLs are employed for the frequency
shift generator (FSK) in order to generate 4.8kHz for a "0" to be recorded,
and 6.4kHz for a "1" to be recorded. The FSK detector detects "1s" and "0s".
The clock generator puts out a clock of 800Hz.

FIGURE 3-9 Block diagram of a phase-lock-loop system for recording and
readback of Manchester code from a cassette.

loop (LP filter, amplifier, VCO, and back to the phase detector). See
Fig. 3-10.

Figure 3-11 shows the detected output of the SKC detector. For a
"1" output a high level of about 60% of the interval in output, or the
"1" level gives an output. For a "0" level there is no output in the bit
interval as is shown in the figure. In other words, 6.4 kHz is detected as
a "1" while 4.8 kHz is detected as a "0" with no output representing
readback of a recorded "0".

The last method for data recording can be described as the pulse-
width method of storing "1s" and "0s". In this method one of two
one-shot multivibrators is triggered by a "1" and the other by a "0".
Each provides a pulse of two different widths as is shown in Fig. 3-12.

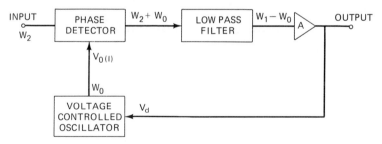

A phase-lock loop system is an electronic serve. A simple method to describe
a phase-lock loop (PLL) is to view the input signal as phase compared to the
output signal. Thus, input and output frequencies are compared and locked
to the input frequency via the path around the loop (LP filter, amplifier,
VCO, and back to the phase detector).

FIGURE 3-10 Block diagram of a phase-lock loop.

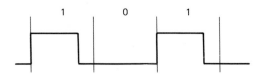

FIGURE 3-11 Data recording by method of Figure 3-9.

These pulses are ORed and sent to a standard head recording circuit as used for Manchester code. The receiving circuit is similar to the Manchester receiving circuit, but with one major difference. The leading edge of each pulse triggers another one-shot, which receivers a reference clock. This one-shot triggers a second one-shot that generates a clock pulse at the middle of the data interval. This pulse is both ANDed directly with the data, and if a "1" is received a flip-flop is set. If a "0" is received the data is inverted and ANDed with the clock but run to the reset side of a flip-flop. In this manner a flip-flop is set and reset by "1", "0" codes and restores digital level data. The transmitter circuit is shown in Fig. 3-13 and the receiver circuit in Fig. 3-14.

All three of these basic methods will record and read data back from a magnetic medium, and the choice of which method to use is a design department decision. Although Manchester code is still the favorite, the pulse-width method has a major advantage of always synchronizing the clock on the leading edge of the data, thus eliminating the necessity of requiring a synchronizing interval before transmitting data.

3-3.2 Incremental Tapes

Paper tape and card equipment's traditional functions of loading and unloading program data now face a new competitor, namely, incremental magnetic tape, which not only reads and writes at speeds

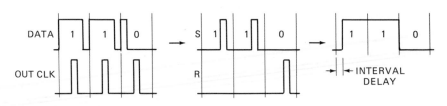

FIGURE 3-12 Pulse-width recording.

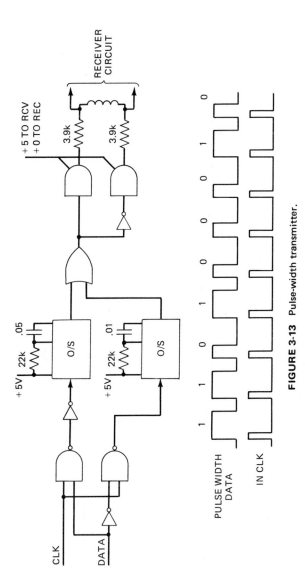

FIGURE 3-13 Pulse-width transmitter.

55

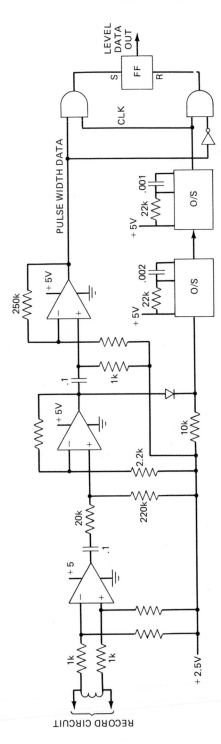

FIGURE 3-14 Pulse-width receiver.

FIGURE 3-15 Incremental magnetic tape reader/recorder. (Courtesy Kennedy Company, California)

equaling paper tape devices but also stores information much more compactly (from 200 to 800 characters per inch). Also, it is usually cost competitive. A typical unit appears in Fig. 3-15.

The incremental magnetic tape transport differs from the conventional magnetic tape transport in that the tape motion stops after the reading or recording of a single character, meaning that during the data-store mode data may be recorded at unequal intervals of time yet the spacing on the tape remains constant. Also, standard IBM formats for magnetic tape may be retained; thus, the incremented tapes can be read on conventional magnetic tape transports of the continuous-run category.

3-3.3 Floppy Disks

The usual disk file, discussed in the next chapter, is an extension of the magnetic drum with a few improvements such as recording 8 bits (1 byte) in parallel, and it is classified as a bulk-store device. The floppy disk is much less expensive than a disk file, since the emergence of the minicomputer and microcomputer. It records serially in groups and records, much like a phonograph record, but the read/write head is normally servoed or are stepping motor positioned to maintain tight track tolerances. In addition to loading/unloading programs, it acts as a form of bulk-store, with an access time greater than cassettes but slower than a normal 8-disk file because of its serial nature. Typical floppy disks now being manufactured are listed in Table 3-5. Figure 3-16 is a photo of such a typical floppy disk unit.

TABLE 3-5
FLOPPY DISK CHARACTERISTICS

Manufacturer	Qume	Calcomp	IBM	Interdata	Pertec	Micropolis
Model	8-dual sided	143M	3740	DS3901	FD250	111-1015
Rotation rate (rpm)	360	360	360	300	300	300
Tracks/in.	—	48	44	—	48	48
Access time (millisec)	10	6	2.5	30	25	30
Record density (bits/in.)	6816	6800	378	5162	5536	5462
Cylinders	77	77	77	128	70	287
Record method	MFM	MFM	MFM	MFM	MFM	MFM
Tracks	154	154	77	1120	—	44
Transfer rate (bits/sec)	500K	500K	250K	61.9K	250K	250K
Dimensions	4.6W×8.6H× 14.6D"	4.9H×8.4W× 15D"	—	10H×11.5W× 13D"	3.3H×5.8W× 8D"	3.4H×5.9W× 8.5D"
Weight	13 lb	16 lb	—	27 lb	3.2 lb	3.9 lb
Total bytes	16m bytes/disk*	8m bytes/disk*	—	143K formatted	457.5K	287K formatted
Power	55 W	196 W	—	125 W	26.5 W	16 W
MTBF**	6000 hr	7000 hr	5000 hr	—	—	8500 hr.
Interface	RS232C	RS232C	RS232C, ASC II	RS232C, ASC II	—	Optional

*1m byte = 1 million bytes.
**MTBF signified Mean Time Between Failures expected in hours.

FIGURE 3-16 A floppy disk unit. (Courtesy Perkin-Elmer Data Systems)

3-3.4 Cassettes

These units are derived from the audio cassette business but use higher quality tape to avoid loss of data bits because of tape imperfections. A photo of a typical cassette unit is shown by Fig. 3-17. Characteristics of a few typical units are outlined in Table 3-6. Cassettes advance serially for reading or writing by command of the computer. They tend to read/write serially in records or files and perform all the functions of paper tape and card devices but obviously are more compact. They do not move data as fast as a floppy disk, but there are also no reel problems as occur with incremental tape devices.

3-3.5 Cartridges

The cartridge is somewhat like the incremental tape, and usually has more than a single track like the cassette. From two to eight tracks are common, but in some cases up to 20 tracks are used. Cartridges are replaceable just as are cassettes. Some systems use 4 two-track cassettes to obtain 8-bit parallel outputs. When these cartridges are driven by the same driver motor there is usually no alignment problem; that is, no misalignment occurs between bits of one character. From 800 to 1600 bits per inch (bpi) are normally employed for tape lengths up to 1000 ft

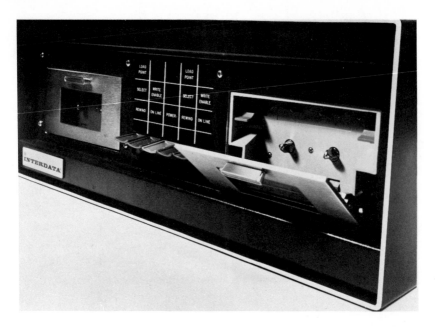

FIGURE 3-17 A cassette unit. (Courtesy Parkin-Elmer Data Systems)

and byte transfers up to 720K bytes/sec for cartridge driven, but these factors can vary widely, depending on track bit densities and the tape speeds used.

3-3.6 Winchester Disk/Cartridge Drive

This is a relatively new device and is best described as a disk and tape cartridge all in the same package. Usually, the disk is 7 to 8 in. in diameter. Rapid data access is from the disk, while the cartridge serves as backup, a place to dump or retrieve data from the disk. This device is more expensive than either a floppy disk or magnetic cartridge, but it does have many applications. In some cases 14 in. disks have been employed. Density of recording and track spacing is the same as for any other disk, but with 8 to 14 in. diameters available, there can be more tracks on a single- or double-sided disk. Several companies manufacture this device, including Onyx Business Systems, Kennedy, Inc., Century Data Systems, and Data Electronics, Inc. The Data Electronics CSR-7000 series backs up a 50m byte disk with 34m bytes on the cartridge. The recording density is high (7200 bpi). Transfer rate from the tape is 200K bits/sec at 30 in./sec. The data rate from the disk is

TABLE 3-6

CHARACTERISTICS OF CASSETTES

Manufacturer	Memodyne	Hewlett-Packard	Facit	Perkins-Elmer	Telex
Model	2333	9875A	4203	Intertape	Terminal 137A
Tracks	8	2 dual cartridges	2	2 dual cartridges	10, 15, or 30 8-bits serial or parallel
Bits/byte	8	8	8	8	8
Ft of tape	270	190	270	270	270
Bits/in.	267	1,600	800	1,000	2,000
Bits/sec	1,600	12,000	3,000 or 6,000	8,000	16,000
Read/write	*	*	*	*	*
Dimension	5H×9W×7.5D"	5.2H×8.4W×13.6D"	6.3H×8.5W×13.3D"	7H×19W×6D" (approx.)	—
Power	7 W	48 W	75 W	151 W (approx.)	—
Recording type	NRZ	Delta dist.	Phase	NRZ	NRZ
Total stored (chars.)	72K	225/cartr.	27K	500K/cartr.	$1.07×10^6$

*Means it is possible to both read and write on same cassette mount.

the same. Up to eight disks can be stacked, raising the total disk storage to 400m bytes.

3-4. OTHER LOADING/UNLOADING DEVICES

3-4.1 Key Tape Equipment

To have an operator key punch a deck of IBM cards and then convert them to magnetic tape would appear to include an unneeded step. Why not prepare a magnetic tape directly from a keyboard? Key tape equipment does precisely that. The operator types the desired material on a digital equipped typewriter. The characters typed are stored directly via an incremental magnetic tape recorder. Thus, a magnetic tape is prepared that can be read directly into the processor via a standard continuous-run transport. Such equipment is illustrated by Fig. 3-18. The operator may verify what is on the tape, either by reading a

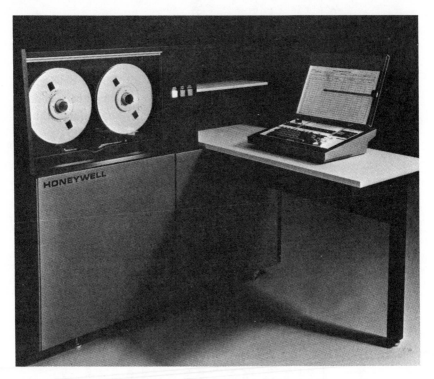

FIGURE 3-18 Key Tape equipment. (Courtesy Data Products Division, Honeywell, Inc.)

printed copy prepared along with the tape or by having the tape replayed to operate the typewriter as a printer.

3-4.2 Key Disk Equipment

This equipment is similar in use to key tape equipment but instead stores data from multiple operators in separate areas of a disk file. Each operator has an individual storage area just as in the key tape case, but the key disk system has the advantage of quicker computer access, which is roughly in the same ratio as the time to access any CRMT message versus a message stored on disk. For the type of disk discussed in Section 4-3 of the next chapter, the access time is in milliseconds, while that of CRMTs is in seconds. ASC II codes are most often employed.

3-4.3 Keyboards

The manual entry of data into a computing system is generally via a keyboard, which may be a separate unit, part of a Teletype, a special typewriter, or one associated with a CRT (see Chapter 5). Keyboards come in a variety of styles, including those having only digits, or digits and alphanumerics, or all the symbols of the ASC II or EBCDIC codes discussed in the Appendix. Pressing a key generates a specific code which is usually stored in a random access memory, buffer registers, etc., until the program is able to digest the code. Keys come in a variety of types, including mechanical, photoelectric, or other special forms of pickups.

3-5 OPTICAL CHARACTER RECOGNITION (OCR)

3-5.1 General

Since much human communication involves documentation, the capability of reading a written page directly into a processor would eliminate such nonproductive operations as first key punching data from documents to IBM cards. Following the key-punch step, the cards are then read into the processor. Much work has been done in the field of direct document reading since the early 1950s, and many efficient machines are on the market and in present use. They vary from relatively inexpensive machines that read a very restrictive font to more versatile ones that read a variety of fonts and even hand-printed symbols in some instances. Because of their function in a system OCRs are sometimes termed *reverse printers*. In general, the equipment is quite expensive, but new developments are reducing its cost.

3-5.2 Methods of Operation

The simplest OCR method is illustrated by Fig. 3-19. Here the character image to be read is projected on a flat surface. Also projected on the same surface selectively are reverse images of all of the fonts for which recognition is anticipated. When the reflected light drops to its low level, as sensed by a photocell, the best match is achieved, and thus the character is recognized. This method is simple but is dependent on an exact registration, not easily achieved. Also, the font is usually restricted to only one type.

A second approach is to selectively scan the character in one direction, perhaps in three or more sweeps. Depending on the character, a distinctive pattern of light and dark areas are sensed. By employing threshold detection, the distinctive areas can be converted to "1" or "0" patterns. By comparing the scanned "1" and "0" patterns with stored patterns, the character scanned is recognized. To avoid resolution problems, the scans must be of a sufficient number to cover areas beyond the character boundaries. The method is illustrated by Fig. 3-20.

The method of scanning varies. Originally, NIPKO disks were pro-

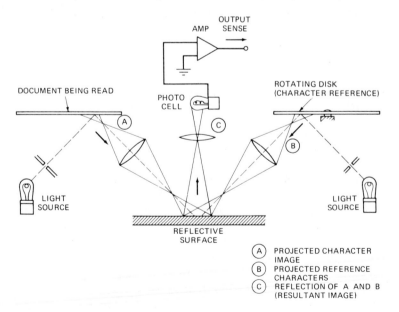

FIGURE 3-19 OCR by matching character masks.

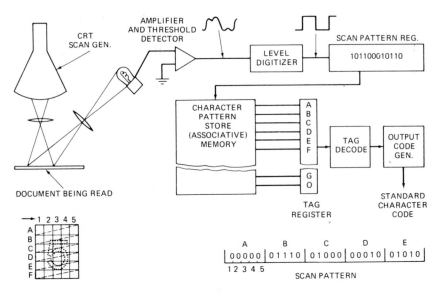

FIGURE 3-20 OCR by scan conversion.

posed, but their mechanical nature decreased their popularity (as did their original proposed use for TV scanning, which never succeeded when proposed by the Bell Telephone Laboratories in the late 1920s).

A more efficient method is to employ a CRT scan converter. This device produces a raster scan, which is projected and reflected to a photocell. The dark areas of the letters (or other characters) are sensed in a time sequence, and a pattern of "1s" and "0s" is again generated via threshold logic.

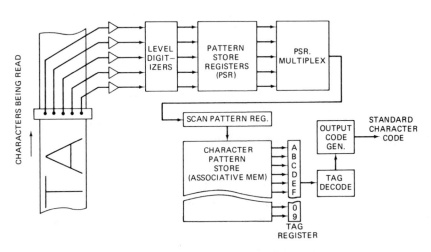

FIGURE 3-21 OCR by photocell method.

Another method to provide the scan is the use of a bank of individual sensors, as shown by Fig. 3-21. Here the moving of the paper, with its characters under the sensing cells, produces a time-dependent waveform which is easily converted to "1s" and "0s".

3-5.3 Problems

OCR devices, although potentially useful now, have been plagued with difficult problems. These include resolution (or how fine must the character be scanned), registration (or how close must the character be aligned with the recording device), and definition (or font identification). In addition, OCR has to contend with imperfect typing, smudges, smears, ink spots, coffee stains, crumpled paper, creases, different colored papers and type, different density of type, specks, and many other things. It's no wonder that efficient, successful, low-cost OCR equipment has been difficult to develop.

3-5.4 A Scan Data Modern Converter for OCR

Scan Data builds an OCR scanner that scans prescribed formats. Their model 410 is a compact, single-line pass OCR system that consists of the scan head, a video processor, font recognition, control logic, and a power supply. The character throughput ranges from 100 to over 1000 characters per second, with a recognition error of about 0.01%.

The system works in general as follows. A document transport system moves a document past the scanning head. The head assembly illuminates the document, and the reflected light from the document is imaged onto a solid-state, 64 photodiode array. The array then produces a series of electrical pulses whose amplitude is a function of the reflected light pattern received. This pattern is detected by the diodes as an analog current and does it in two horizontal sensing strips 0.4 in. high. Each pulse represents the amplitude of the image at that point. A video amplifier converts these current pulses to a voltage which is later digitized in the video processor to represent the black and white areas of the character. Although only two levels are scanned, this enhances character recognition sufficiently despite smears and lines slightly displaced from the ideal. Thus, patterns can be compared with those stored and the process does its job, by shifting the pattern obtained through a shift register.

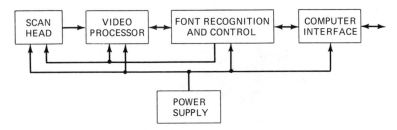

FIGURE 3-22 The Scan Data method in block diagram form.

The control logic generates shift pulses, strobing, and clock signals for the scan arrays, character-positioning space recognition, valid recognition, and character decoding with the stored pattern so that recognition is finalized.

The interface logic receives and transmits the input/output and can be RS232C, ASC II, or a customer specified format. The dc power supply provides all the power to the 410 unit. The one described here is shown in Fig. 3-22. A few samples of fonts are illustrated in Fig. 3-23. Figure 3-24 is a photo of a scan head.

This OCR detector is not the entire process. Equipment using this converter can decode a print or display a document on a CRT. Or it could well be part of a transmission system using an ASC II format or RS232C. The devices are linked to tape or disk equipment and are used in government, business, and in industry. This particular scanner is a vast improvement over those of the early 1970s.

FIGURE 3-23 Some typical formats read by the 410. (Courtesy Scan Data Corp.)

FIGURE 3-24 Scan head. (Courtesy Scan Data Corp.)

3-6 COMPUTER RECOGNITION OF SPEECH

This is a brand new approach for inputting data and (1980) is in the research stage at laboratories such as Bell and (IBM). Automatic speech recognition is presently entering a critical stage. While users of earlier systems are assessing the benefits and weighing them against costs, researchers are exploring even more advanced systems. Development of new systems is not going to be easy, since there are many unknowns yet to explore—all the way from the basics of human perception of language to the access of large associative memory data bases, the selection of storage, and comparisons of features of speech.

Even if the researchers are proven wrong, one thing is clear: the technology is moving toward making computers available to people without special skills. Speech is our most common method of communication. Unlike keyboards and other apparatus, direct speech requires no special skills or training. It allows the talker to be mobile and/or remote from the computer input terminal, and it permits use of the talker's hands and eyes for other aspects of a task.

Speech recognition researchers eagerly await large, low-cost, data-processing power accessible by very large-scale integrated devices. Many think this, rather than basic knowledge, is what is needed to leap into the era of communication with computers by natural, conversational speech.

Speech input is almost twice as fast as entry by a skilled typist. With speech input, a data-processing system can eliminate intermediate data preparation and entry steps.

Development is proceeding in Japan and France also. Some systems recognize a few words, while others are attempting to recognize words within continuous speech. This latter factor is more difficult to provide reliable devices for, because many people slur words together, which tends to make detailed word recognition harder to provide.

Several devices are already on the market. Although many techniques are potentially available, the one now most common converts analog voice to a digital pattern of "1s" and "0s" and compares this statistically to stored word patterns and selects the one for the best match. Basically, computers are still too slow and expensive. Ten years ago, the early 1970s' computers were too slow even to carry out research in speech recognition.

Still, research continues to better understand the basics of speech, to better separate words, and to develop better tools for the future. Bell and other laboratories are also researching methods to allow computers to reply to a user with simulated speech. Machines that generate simulated speech are just now (1981) emerging from the laboratories.

3-7 SUMMARY

This chapter first covers loading and unloading methods and devices, starting with paper tape punches and readers, which is followed by Hollerith card readers and punches. Both of these types of Hollerith equipment still have wide usage, but the tendency is toward magnetic tape devices, including incremental tapes, floppy disks, cassettes, key tape, key disks, and OCRs of various and improving types. Many photos are included as well as tables that list the characteristics of incremental tapes, floppy disks, cassettes, paper tape, and card equipment. Devices to accept spoken commands are now under development. These are examples of the versatility being planned for the future.

4

Bulk-store
Peripherals

Bulk-storage devices generally provide supplementary data storage external to a processor's internal memory. Bulk-storage apparatus would include continuous-run magnetic tapes (CRMTs), magnetic drums, magnetic disk files (including the newer and less expensive floppys), magnetic cores, magnetic domains (bubble memories), charge-coupled devices (CCDs), computed-operated microfilm (COM), and probably the new silicon disks (which at present are being developed as television storage mediums). There will surely be other developments, but it is difficult to predict their nature in the future.

4-1 CONTINUOUS-RUN MAGNETIC TAPE (CRMT)

This form of bulk-store has been around for many years and is still the least costly on a per bit basis. It is typified by reels of magnetic tape in which characters are recorded as code groups across the tape in a format similar to paper tape, but magnetic spots replace the holes of paper

TABLE 4-1

IBM STANDARD SEVEN-CHANNEL MAGNETIC TAPE FORMATS
AND SPECIFICATIONS

1. *Number of tracks*[c]	*7 data, 1 check bit*
2. *Character density*	*200, 556, 800, 1600 bits per inch*
3. *Data format*	*Binary or character*
4. *Type of recording*	*NRLZ*[a] *(Ferranti) two-gap heads (write/read)*
5. *Tape speed*	*75 or 112.5 in. per second; rewind, 500 in. per second*
6. *Error check*	*Vertical: odd parity for each character*
	Horizontal: odd parity for record of each track Check of character (LRCC[b]*) recorded in EOR gap*
7. *Groupings*	*Record: group of words endings in $\frac{3}{4}$ in. wide gap (EOR)*
	File: group of records ending in $3\frac{1}{2}$ in. wide gap and/or tape mark character (EOF)
8. *End-of-tape mark*	*$\frac{3}{16}$ by 1 in. aluminum strip, 10 ft from tape end, sensed to stop unit*
9. *Tape-capstan start/stop time*	*Less than 3 msec*

[a] NRLZ—Designation for Ferranti, or Manchester, recording code.
[b] LRCC—Designation of parity check character-recorded in end-of-record (EOR) gap.
[c] For EBCDIC code, 8 bits plus 1 check bit are required. Thus 9 tracks is also a standard tape.

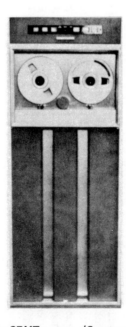

FIGURE 4-1 View of a CRMT system. (Courtesy Honeywell, Inc.)

TABLE 4-2

CHARACTERISTICS OF TYPICAL CRMTS

Manufacturer	Perkins-Elmer		Cypher[a]	Pertec	
Model	M11	M14	Low Profile	T6000	T9000
Tracks	7 or 9	9	9	7 or 9	7 or 9
7-track chars./in. (IBM format)	6 data and 1 check bit: 200, 556, or 800 bits/in.				
9-track chars./in. (IBM format)	8 data (ASC II) and 1 parity check bit: 800 or 1600 bits/in.				
Rewind speed (in./sec)	200	500	100	150	200
Buffer	Yes	Yes	Yes	—	—
Reel size	$10\frac{1}{2}$	$10\frac{1}{2}$	$10\frac{1}{2}$	$10\frac{1}{2}$	$10\frac{1}{2}$
Record speed (in./sec)	75	125	25 or 100	45	75
Record method	Phase[b]	Phase[b]	Phase[b]	Phase[b]	Phase[b]
Vacuum columns	Yes	Yes	No	No	Yes
Dimensions	Std. rack wide	Std. rack wide	8.8H×17W×22D"	—	—
Weight	—	—	50 lb	—	—

[a] 1600 bits/in. only.
[b] Sometimes called Manchester encoding.

tape. In general, the industry has standardized on the IBM format (Table 4-1). The unique characteristics of CRMT is that data is recorded in blocks called *records*. A CRMT system is shown in Fig. 4-1. Characteristics of typical CRMTs are listed in Table 4-2.

Groups of records are called *files*. Data transfers to and from the processor and CRMT are restricted to records and files; that is, individual stand-alone characters are not forwarded. Between successive records in the file there are distinctive gaps in the recordings (see Table 4-1). These are necessary, since the machine reads and records continuously—not intermittently like incremental magnetic tape devices as discussed in Chapter 3. In addition, end-of-file (EOF) and end-of-record (EOR) characters may be recorded. The gaps, however, serve to allow the tape to increase or decrease in speed between records where the tape motion ceases. The EOF space is even greater than the EOR.

The tape transport mechanism is characterized by reels to hold used and unused tape. In addition, there is a capstan to drive the tape at a constant speed across the read/write heads and a mechanism to control slack between the reels and the capstan.

4-2 MAGNETIC DRUMS

On most of the early computers of the 1950s and 1960s this form of bulk store was the most popular and the first to be put in service on early Burroughs computers as a main memory. However, in 1952 a magnetic drum used as a bulk-store on EDVAC was put into operation. Since the EDVAC word was 40 bits it had to be recorded serially. There was a read/write head for each track. A problem developed when the drum speed reached 3300 rpm. The heads heated up so that the plastic mountings expanded, and since the heads themselves moved, the centrifical force plus the plastic expansion was enough to cause the heads to physically contact the surface. This action caused scratches on the surface. As a result future designs had the heads float a few microinches off the surface. This technique became known as *floating heads*. Since the drum does not have greater utility than the disk file, its use has for all practical purposes been abandoned.

4-3 DISK FILES

Disk files perform a function similar to drums but are organized with coaxial data tracks. One form of disk file has a head for every track and is thus functionally identical to a drum. Another form of disk file contains a bank of heads that each read or write one track at a time

FIGURE 4-2 Removable-pack disk file. (Courtesy IBM Corp.)

concurrently on four to eight disks. Thus, an individual character code may be spread between several disks but will have a common corresponding track position on each disk. The arm holding the heads is positioned by a servo under control-positioning instructions from the processor. In addition, the stack of disks is usually replaceable, which allows the operator to replace disk packs in the same manner as tapes are replaced during their use. Figure 4-2 shows this latter type of disk file.

As indicated in Section 3-3.3, floppy disks are not only used as loading/unloading devices but are replacing many of the types shown in Fig. 4-2, since their cost is lower and their reliability improving constantly. In Table 4-3 several typical disk file characteristics are specified.

4-4 MAGNETIC CORES

In the late 1950s and throughout the 1960s all high-speed parallel computers employed magnetic cores for their internal memories, directly addressable by a program. Thousands of these machines are still in service, but in the early 1970s the cores received some real competition from semiconductor memories. Now new computers of all sizes are

TABLE 4-3

CHARACTERISTICS OF DISK DRIVES

Manufacturer	Perkins-Elmer		Hewlett-Packard		PerSci
Model	MSM300	MSM180	7925	7920	277
Total storage (M/bytes)	256	67.2	125	120	50
Formatted (std. IBM)	Yes	Yes	Yes	Yes	Yes
rpm (speed)	3600	3600	2700	3600	360
Disks	12	5	—	—	8 (4 duals)
Transfer rate (M/bytes per sec)	1.2	1.2	0.94	0.94	—
Sectors/track	533	366	64	48	3.3
Bytes/sector	67	46	256	256	128
Tracks	40	40	815	815	77
Weight (lb)	—	—	345	355	20
Power (W)	—	—	550	600	28
Dimensions	—	—	38H×14.7W×32D"	32.5H×19.7W×32D"	8.6H×15W×4.4D"

designed that use semiconductor memories having various characteristics. They are faster, less expensive, and easier to match to the remainder of the computer's logic. Core memories are still employed in
new designs as a bulk-store peripheral. They are much faster to access
than disk files, still following the random-access concept (about to be
described), and their operation is thoroughly understood.

As will be indicated, a "1" is stored as a magnetic flux in the core
of one direction. A "0" is stored as a magnetic flux in the opposite
direction. Wires through the individual cores provide the reading and
writing operation, but special electronics is involved to provide the
proper levels for writing and reading, and these are outlined in this
section.

The bulk-store memory still consists of a magnetic core stack and
associated electronics. This type of memory is termed *random access*,
which means that each stored word is retrievable with equal facility or
that it is possible to store a word at any address with equal ease. There
are no prescribed hardware constraints or fixed sequences in which
words must be addressed by the program. Usually, the addressing order
is determined by the program.

The stack is comprised of magnetic cores connected by wires
which perform the read and write functions. The usual physical configuration provides an individual plane for each bit of the computer
word. There are as many planes as there are word bits. The number of
bits per plane is identical to the number of words stored in the stack. A
typical core plane is illustrated by Fig. 4-3. A complete memory hard-

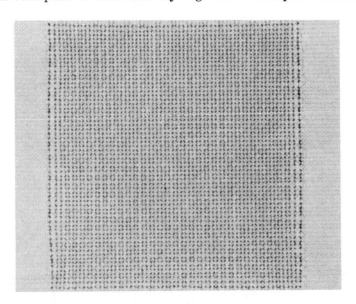

FIGURE 4-3 A typical core plane.

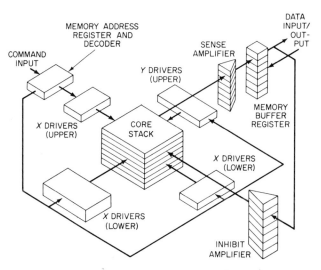

FIGURE 4-4 Core-memory block diagram.

ware package (both stack and electronics) is shown by Fig. 4-4, an exploded diagram. The principles involved here are identical to the original computer internal core memory.

The electronics provides the functions of reading and writing in the cores of the selected word. One core per plane is chosen by the orthogonal X and Y driver lines. The driver lines are pulsed by switching circuits that provide the proper switching current levels and polarities to perform either a read or write.

During the read process a selected core in each plane is sensed by the plane sense amplifiers for a stored "1" or "0". If the plane reads a "1" the memory buffer register (MBR) flip-flop sensing this plane is set. If a "0" is read the flip-flop remains reset. The selected word contents now rests in the MBR and can be transferred elsewhere within the processor. In some memory systems, namely, those featuring a destructive readout of the cores, the contents of the MBR is immediately read back to the cores. Actually, here a "0" in the MBR does not allow a "1" to be written back in the core. A "0" is said to "inhibit" the write "1" process during the restoration of the word in the cores. The MBR is also employed similarly during the write process. Here the new word to be written in the core is deposited just in the MBR. The inhibition of the write "1" process occurs in the same manner for writing "0s" as for the read/restore routine outlined above.

The other register of importance in the memory section is the memory address register (MAR). This register holds the address bits identifying the address of the word cell to be read or written into. The binary address held in the MAR is, in turn, decoded to select the re-

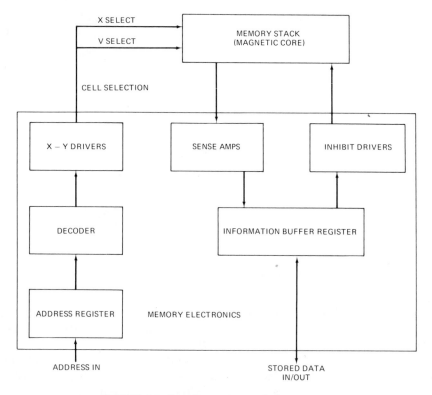

FIGURE 4-5 Data flow and control of a memory.

quired X and Y drivers that physically select the individual word requested. A simplified block diagram of a memory appears in Fig. 4-5.

Memories are generally provided in modular sizes such as 1024, 4096, 8192, and 16,384 words, etc. Larger memories are normally built up from the smaller modules. The modules employed contain both the stack and electronics and occasionally a power supply. Modular sizes 4096 and 8192 are commonly used to construct the larger memories. Word length is varied by selecting the number of planes. Incidentally, 1024 is abbreviated as 1K, 4096 as 4K, 8192 as 8K, and so on.

4-5 SEMICONDUCTOR MEMORIES

With the development of high-density, large-scale integrated (LSI) circuits, it is now both economically and technically feasible to build memories in circuit logic form. Before the advent of this technology, the core and plated-wire forms ruled practically unchallenged except in specialized cases. Beginning in 1971–72, semiconductor memories began to openly challenge the magnetic types that were the standard for over a decade and a half.

There are basically two forms which a random-access LSI memory can take. One is the *static cell* type, where bits are stored in a form of flip-flop. If these cells are of the MOS-FET variety, there is probably a need to refresh their contents, since some MOS-FET cells store "1s" and "0s" as capacitive charges and tend to discharge with time.

A second type is the *dynamic form*, where the stored data is recirculated back into itself, as via a shift register. This, of course, can be organized as a shift of a few bits in sequence and, in effect, is a form of delay line, or the cells can periodically recirculate on themselves (sort of an individual 1-bit delay line).

The advantages of semiconductor or random-access memories lie in their promise of less expensive and faster access memories. Since the elements are effectively I-Cs they interface CPU logic with less com-

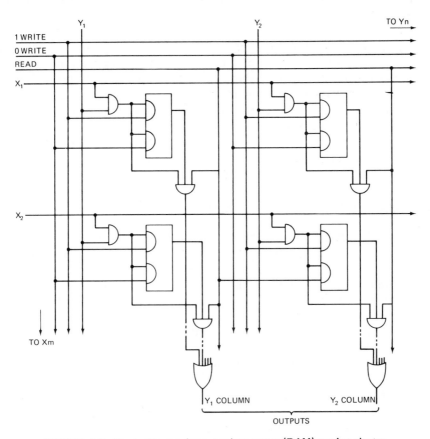

FIGURE 4-6 Block diagram for a random-access (RAM) semiconductor memory.

plexity and usually reduce the need for unique, special power sources for the memory stack itself. I-C element forms can be attractive for memory applications. Other developments in the semiconductor memory field, such as charge-coupled devices (CCD), appear to offer great potential for the future. A simplified block diagram for a semiconductor random-access memory (RAM) is shown in Fig. 4-6.

Bipolar I-Cs, although faster than MOS devices, have the disadvantage of occupying more chip space per element. But with I^2L and H-MOS there is an improvement in reduction of the memory chip element's size. It is well known that MSIs and LSIs, when used in memory chips along with C-MOS, reduce overall power requirements. Actually, either bipolar or unipolar devices are fabricated in dozens of units per board. They are structured in many combinations, such as 4096 × 1 bit or 512 × 2 bits or 256 × 4 bits. Therefore, a 16 bit by 4096 would take 16 dips, a 16 bit by 8192 would take 32 dips; however, with the advent of I^2L and H-MOS, density increases of 10 to 1 are possible. Future projections indicate even greater increases in densities, such as 64K bits/chip.

In any semiconductor memory a word to be accessed or written in must be addressed just as in a magnetic core memory. Since a word consists of a number of bits there must be a corresponding number of line drivers (X-Y) and a bit recorder for each bit common to the word to sense a "1" or "0". For this reason we need a memory address register (MAR) and a memory buffer register (MBR). These registers, along with read and write strobes, perform the same functions as they do for a magnetic core memory; however, they can generally be logic levels, rather than special high-current pulses.

4-6 MAGNETIC BUBBLE MEMORY

A new 92K-bit magnetic bubble memory was introduced by Texas Instruments in April, 1977. The principle of operation of a bubble memory is shown in Fig. 4-7. Bits to be stored (bubbles) originate in the bubble generator and are passed via a one-way generator lock to the major loop. Bit distance p determines the maximum number of serial bits in the major loop between successive and adjacent minor loops (L_1 to L_n). Minor loops permit circulation in one direction only, controllable by a rotating magnetic field. Reversing magnetic fields at the proper time permits switching word strings in or out of a minor loop to the major loop. Data readout is via the annihilator lock of the bubble annihilator. Access time for any word requires several milliseconds. A 92K-bit memory is now available, with 1 million-bit memories expected soon. There are 661 bubble positions in each of 157 minor loops (100,657 bits), but allowance must be made for 8% of such loops being defective, thus reducing the 157 figure to 144, yielding about 92K bits.

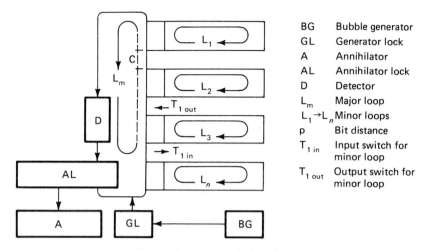

BG	Bubble generator
GL	Generator lock
A	Annihilator
AL	Annihilator lock
D	Detector
L_m	Major loop
$L_1 \rightarrow L_n$	Minor loops
p	Bit distance
$T_{1\,in}$	Input switch for minor loop
$T_{1\,out}$	Output switch for minor loop

FIGURE 4-7 Functioning of a bubble memory.

The cycle for the 144-bit page is 12.8 millisec; thus, it is anticipated that bubble memories will soon compete with disks and drums having access to CCD memories, which at present are 1000 times faster than bubble memories. Newer magnetic bubble memories contain over a megabit of data.

4-7 CHARGE-COUPLED DEVICES (CCD)

Although disk files and magnetic tape units have traditionally provided bulk storage, some of the newer developing technologies appear to offer improved capabilities. In the early computers data storage involved rotating bits (for example, in a drum computer). CCDs have been updated to include CCD shift registers, which are ideally suited to this memory technique since they are temperature insensitive (and since mercury delay lines are not). CCDs essentially store electrons in potential wells (regions near a semiconductor's surface). Once the charge is stored it can be transported by applying voltages between adjacent electrodes. Thus, as for a logic shift register, "1s" and "0s" can be shifted from the first cell to the final cell in successive steps. This storage process continues by tying the output to the input (recirculation) and by reading an output from the last stage. A CCD can be designed so that many parallel data streams can be recirculated simultaneously. By this technique a complete character code or word can be shifted at each clock time.

Advantages of this kind of storage over mechanical storage should be self-evident: there are no large rotating disks with mechanical movements. CCD units are compact, accommodating over 200,000 bits per

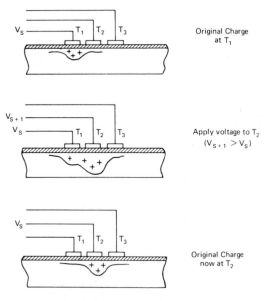

FIGURE 4-8 Principles of CCD.

square inch. Recirculation time is at the machine's clock rate. At present these devices are being offered by suppliers in reasonable quantities, and research is continuing. An example of their operation is shown in Fig. 4-8.

4-8 MICROFILM STORE

A relatively inexpensive way to store documentation would be to combine the processes of microfilm with a processor index. Thus, the processor would locate a microfilm document record, retrieve it, and display it on a suitable viewer, such as a CRT. The process involves the operator punching the document's address on a keyboard, so that when it is positioned, it will be scanned and a digital code will be generated. This equipment allows the operator to view the actual microfilm, lessening the need for disk-file storage. However, the mechanical actuation of a viewer cartridge leads to some interesting mechanical problems— about the magnitude of a sophisticated automated record–player jutebox. The system is blocked out in Fig. 4-9. The name commonly attached to this equipment is Computer Operated Microfilm (COM).

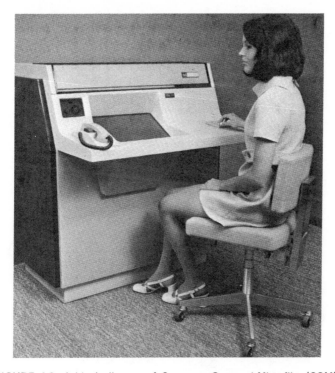

FIGURE 4-9 A block diagram of Computer Operated Microfilm (COM) system.

4-9 A COMPARISON OF MAGNETIC BULK STORE

A gross comparison of bulk-store devices is shown in Table 4-4. Generally, magnetic tapes store data in a less costly form, but the access to a given list of data is rather slow. There is usually no addressing of the records, although that can be done by starting each record with a recognizable code, thus permitting a program instruction to compare with a reference.

Drums and separate head-per-track disks are functionally identical and have the fastest access time of any magnetic-mechanical form of storage. The individual tracks as well as the data's circumferential position on a track can be addressed. Usually, data can also be transferred in record groups.

Another form of disk file utilizes head groups that are servo positioned to a selected track. Again, the positioning is addressable, and the transfer is in record groups. This form of disk file is slower to access then the head-per-track type due to the requirement of first positioning the heads of the latter. Access, however, is normally faster than for

TABLE 4-4
COMPARISON OF MAGNETIC BULK-STORE DEVICES

	Storage (bits)	Transfer (chars./sec)	Density (chars./in.)	Average Access	Approx. Cost ($/bit)
1. *Magnetic tape:*					
Continuous-run	16.1×10^7	56K	800	125 sec	0.0015
Incremental	8.1×10^7	2K	800	48 min	0.00005
Cassette	3.6×10^6	4K	180	300 sec	0.001
2. *Rotating:*					
Drums	1.5×10^6	300K	500	8 millisec	0.015
Disk file (fixed-head)	5.0×10^6	300K	1000	8 millisec	0.005
Disk file (moveable head)	2.0×10^6	200K	500	200 millisec	0.010
3. *Magnetic core:*	16.0×10^6	120K	—	8 microsec	0.05

TABLE 4-5

IMPORTANT FEATURES OF MAGNETIC BULK-STORE DEVICES

A. *Magnetic tape:*
  1. *Usable for:*
     (a) *Occasionally accessed bulk store (where low cost per bit is important)*
     (b) *Load and unload main processor memory*
     (c) *Where tapes must be replaceable*
  2. *Transfer characteristics:*
     (a) *Multiwords in records or files*
     (b) *Via buffered channel (DMA)*
B. *Disk files:*
  1. *Usable for:*
     (a) *Data to be accessed often*
     (b) *Moderate cost for storage ($/bit)*
     (c) *Some forms of disks replaceable*
  2. *Transfer characteristics:*
     (a) *Multiwords in records or files*
     (b) *Via buffered channel (DMA)*
C. *Magnetic core:*
     (a) *Single-word access (via DIO)*
     (b) *Relatively fast access*
     (c) *Expensive on a per bit basis*

magnetic tape and has the advantage over the fixed-head disk in the replaceability of the disk packs themselves. Thus, this feature acquires one of the advantages of replaceable magnetic tapes.

Floppy disks are now recognized forms of bulk store, especially for mini- and microcomputers. The cassette has rather limited capacity as a bulk-store device, but in a few selected instances, such as storing special programs or data, they may have the necessary capabilities. Comparisons of model characteristics of floppy disks are shown in Table 3-5. Table 4-5 lists important bulk-store features.

4-10 SUMMARY

In this chapter we summarize the more common bulk-store devices, except for the silicon disk, which is covered in a limited manner in Chapter 9. Some devices, such as cassette storage and the floppy disk, can be included in either loading/unloading devices or as bulk store, depending on how they are used in a system; it is common practice to use these latter devices in both modes. We chose to include these in Chapter 3.

Generally, bulk store supplements main internal memory by providing extra storage space. For example, other programs can be stored in bulk store and dumped into main memory whenever a program calls for the data. At the same time, the old program can be transferred for storage to the bulk-store unit. A new standard tape code, EBCDIC, is shown in Appendix Table A-7.

Some of the original data storage approaches now seem quite crude. At one time, Teletype tapes or Hollerith cards were the only I/O available. That era was followed by a series of experimental devices. For example, magnetic card shufflers and slotted-disk memories that were never produced commercially. Immediately after World War II magnetic drums were used both as a main memory and as a bulk-store peripheral. After the 1960s drums were almost entirely replaced by disk files. Because of their high cost original peripheral processing equipment such as large expensive drums and disks have been replaced by floppy disks and cassettes. Probably, the first attempt to use magnetized wire for voice recording occurred during World War II. This was a total failure, so emphasis turned to magnetic tape and magnetic drums.

Other new approaches include the magnetic bubble, charge-coupled devices (CCD), silicon disks, and computer-operated microfilm (COM). There are many other approaches, including differing storage materials and possibly even holograms, the latter used to transmit three-dimensional images. Magnetic bubbles and CCD are very fast compared to magnetic devices and are possible future replacements. Momentarily, silicon disks are at a disadvantage, not being erasable, but they are described briefly in Chapter 9.

5

Display Peripherals

5-1 GENERAL

Display peripherals consist of equipment that displays data for interpretation by an observer. These devices include printers of various types, cathode-ray tube displays (CRTs), and plotters, which produce curves or graphs depicting business or experimental information. One such graph plots data versus time. Another plots data in coordinate form (left-right and up-down). Known as an X-Y plotter, the device moves a stylus under servo control in two right-angle directions.

Sometimes plotters and printers can be incorporated as one device; in fact, an early plotter, using a Teletype mechanism printer, plots by printing "Xs" as the paper is moved from line to line. Another form of plotter with closely spaced stylusus probes spread across a page also serves as a printer. This chapter concerns these kinds of devices.

5-2 METHODS OF PRINTING

The earliest printing technique involved a hammer with an imprinted character striking against a ribbon adjacent to the paper, similar to a typewriter mechanism. Another approach was to ink a metal drum, containing rows of each letter of the alphabet across the drum. For each line to be printed the drum made one revolution, and simultaneously, all the desired characters were struck by column hammers. After a single revolution of the drum, a line would be completely printed, and the paper would move to the next line. A mechanism of this nature was first developed by Frank Sheppard and marketed by the Vogue Instrument Company. This kind of printer is known as a *line printer*, since a parallel line is printed during one revolution of a printing drum. It is a relatively fast form of printing. Teletypes and other printers which print one character at a time, from left to right, are much slower, but for monitoring and because of their relatively low cost they have been widely used. These are known as *character printers*.

Another method employs a dot matrix of 5 × 7 in. or other dimensions. Printing is accomplished by mechanical striking, thermal heating, or generating an electric arc, etc. An electronic character generator is employed to actuate the matrix head for the desired character.

A third method is a variation of the previous one. To print characters the proper strobes are excited, and then the paper is advanced one-seventh of a character's height, if a 5 × 7 dot matrix is employed. Then the advance to the next line to be printed occurs. This type device was probably pioneered by Gould, Inc.; it also doubles as a plotter.

A fourth method has been employed for extremely high-speed printing, where an entire page is displayed on a cathode-ray tube and then exposed to sensitive paper. This method is used infrequently.

In a fifth method the characters are spaced on a rotating chain that moves parallel to the line being printed. The characters for the entire line are stored in a buffer. When a character is in the desired position, a hammer for each column strikes the character against a ribbon; thus, the characters are imprinted on the paper, printing an entire line. This method is called *chain printing*, an alternative to impact printing employing a drum.

A sixth method was devised originally by Western Electric about 1970. IBM is now marketing this system, whereby individual characters are formed from charged electrodes, directing a stream of ink to form the desired characters in sequence.

5-3 PRINTERS

5-3.1 Low-Speed Printers

The alphanumeric form of printout is probably the most common form of processor output. Nowhere in the peripheral field are there more variations than among printers. As an example, there is the processor typewriter, which is essentially a typewriter modified to accept alphanumeric codes from the processor that actuate the letter key mechanism via decoders and solenoids. The keyboard can also serve as an input device. However, because of relatively slow character speed (10 to 30 characters per second) the typewriter form of input/output is used only for the most modest of installations.

However, a processor-connected typewriter is often part of a control console and is used to print diagnostic or log-type messages for operators or to serve as a control input by an operator. Typewriters and Teletype printer/keyboards serve the same functions. Quite often, they are also equipped with slow-speed paper tape handling gear, that is, paper tape readers and paper tape punches that also operate at the same speed and in parallel with the print operation.

Another minimal form of printer is the *strip printer*. This device prints a single strip of alphanumeric characters in much the same manner as composed for the old-fashioned telegram. The strip printer also operates at relatively slow speeds, 10 characters per second or thereabouts.

5-3.2 High-Speed Printers

The high-speed printer is typified by the so-called *line printer*. This device prints an entire line (80 to 130 characters) virtually immediately. It prints upward of 60 lines per second and is in some cases even faster.

The mechanism is basically a drum containing all the character fonts on a single wheel for each column. Thus, for a 120 column printer there would be 120 character wheels. The characters for the line to be printed are stored in a character buffer within the printer. The 120 hammers selectively tap on the paper when the selected character for each column appears underneath the hammer as the wheels (now called a *drum*) rotate. Note that for a particular line

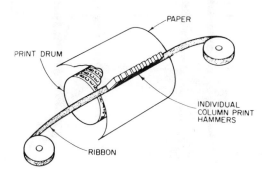

FIGURE 5-1 Drum printing mechanism.

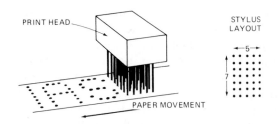

FIGURE 5-2 Matrix printing head.

all *A*s are printed, followed by all *B*s, followed by all *C*s, etc. The drum rotates once for each line. After the line is printed, the paper moves up one line and is positioned for the hammering out of the next line during the next rotation of the character drum. Figure 5-1 illustrates the concept for this form of mechanical printing.

Dot matrix printing requires a print matrix, as illustrated by Fig. 5-2. The mechanism for printing, as previously mentioned, is by pressure, applying heat (thermal), or by electronic means such as striking an arc. Typical matrix printers are shown in Figs. 5-3 and 5-4. In this form of line printer the paper is advanced one line after completion of the previous line of the printing process.

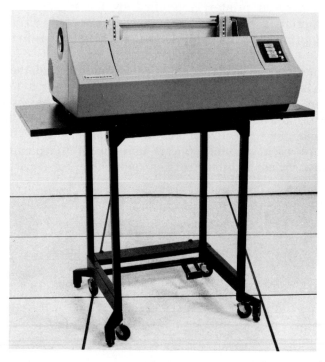

FIGURE 5-3 Matrix printer (Courtesy Perkins-Elmer Data Systems).

FIGURE 5-4 Matrix printer (Courtesy C. Itoh Electronics, Inc.).

5-3.3 Extremely High-speed Method
of Printing

This method utilizes a special character-forming CRT tube. The line to be printed is formed by temporarily storing characters (in fact a whole page) glowing on the face of a CRT tube. Sensitive paper is exposed to these characters and then in turn exposed to light for a few seconds, causing the printout to develop. This system provides extremely high printout rates relatively inexpensively, but the quality of the printout is sometimes blurred at the highest speeds. Figure 5-5 illustrates this particular system.

5-4 CATHODE-RAY TUBE DISPLAYS (CRTs)

When fast access to data and charts is essential, a CRT display serves as an ideal device. As indicated in the previous section, sometimes CRT displays may be employed, in conjunction with sensitized paper exposure, as a plotter or extremely high-speed printer. Often, CRTs are equipped with an alphanumeric keyboard and so serve as an input device for data also. Thus, alphanumerics, graphs, charts, and mechanical or electrical drawings may be presented. By a device called a *light pen*, these drawings can be modified and then the new designs may

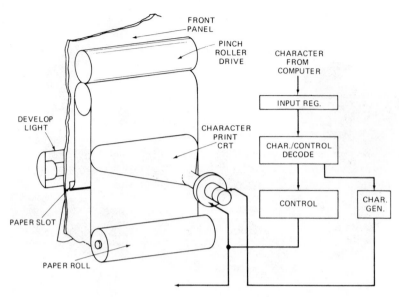

FIGURE 5-5 CRT printing mechanism.

be stored in the computer memory or stored in another peripheral device for later recall. Figure 5-6 illustrates a CRT display, including a keyboard. For air traffic control or weapon targeting displays, for example, these CRT displays ease the solution of difficult control problems. Table 5-2 (p. 99) lists characteristics of some typical commercial and military units.

There are three modes of operation for displaying data on a CRT screen. The first method involves display of alphanumeric or other symbols. The most common approach employs a character generator which is commanded to wiggle a beam to trace out a desired character or symbol on the screen. For example, the electronic beam may initially be positioned at the upper left-hand corner of the screen, and then a complete page may be formed, character by character, line by line. Characters are traced on short segments or possibly as a dot matrix, and perhaps by shining the beam through pattern generators, where each character is scanned first through a template and then onto the CRT. The main beam follows the lines and skips down to the next lower one, but returns to the left-hand side of the screen before starting a new line. The minimum number of template characters is usually 64 but may be several more if both lower- and upper-case displays are necessary.

In many systems the beam is initially positioned by magnetic deflection and the characters themselves shaped by electrostatic signals applied to character-shaping plates. Sometimes the character is traced by placing a "1" in each position that is to bear a mark. Thus, even

Japanese or Chinese characters are available. Six-bit codes allow up to 64 characters, 8-bit codes up to 256, etc.

Some typical components of CRT display systems involve the character generators just mentioned, as well as the following components.

1. *Vector generator*: This component draws lines on the scope, their length and direction depending on a starting and ending location address. Curved lines can be drawn as a connected group of straight lines having overlapping starting and stopping addresses.

2. *Light pen or light gun*: This device picks up light from the CRT screen when pressed against the screen's surface. The pen or gun is used to indicate a point for interrogation or to indicate to the system a point the instruction refers to.

3. *Keyboard*: This device, along with the control keys and light pen, is the primary communication device of the display. The keyboard allows an operator to enter data, for example, a letter or document for editing. The probability is that the keyboard will have both alphanumeric symbols and some system control capability, as well as special symbols.

Although these devices are typical, there are many other features of modern equipment, including color, the capability of adding addi-

FIGURE 5-6   A CRT display unit including an alphanumeric keyboard. (Courtesy Sperry Corp., Sperry Univac Division.)

tional background information (such as photos or movies), the capability of making a recording at some time in the future, and the generation of special displays (such as circles or other geometric shapes), symbols that flicker, as well as changes to existing displays such as typical design drawings. Views can be shown from different directions to simulate three dimensions.

5-5 PLOTTERS

5-5.1 Roll Plotters

There are basically three kinds of plotters. The first is one where the pen or stylus is center-positioned if an input signal is at a "0" level, to the right if positive, and to the left if negative, the amount of deviation being proportional to the signal amplitude. As long as the pen is positioned, the paper rolls underneath; thus, the plot shown is signal amplitude versus time. Plotters manufactured by firms such as Esterline-Angus and General Electric are good examples of this device.

The modern trend is to replace the pen or stylus by closely spaced probes, as mentioned in the section on printers. The paper still moves beneath the probes, and individual probes are actuated in the proper sequence to delineate the desired plot. As indicated in Sections 5-2 and 5-3, printer/plotter combinational devices are now available. Table 5-3 (p. 100) lists several types of plotters and their characteristics.

5-5.2 X-Y Plotters

For this type of plotter the surface of the plotter is flat and stationary. A stylus is servoed individually in both the X and Y directions (left-right and up-down). Servos are relatively complex and expensive devices, so the modern trend is to replace them with less-expensive stepping motors which are digitally controlled. The desired X position is stored in a counter, and each time the motor steps, moving the stylus, a "1" is subtracted from the counter. When the count is "0", the stepping motor stops, the stylus having moved to the desired position. Again, separate X and Y systems are provided, and each works in the same manner. Rapid advances in microprocessor manufacture are lowering the cost of plotters as well as virtually all other peripherals.

5-5.3 CRT Plotters

These devices appeared in the early 1970s as high-speed printers. For permanent copies they are not very popular because of the necessity to develop sensitized paper. Where Polaroid-type film can be

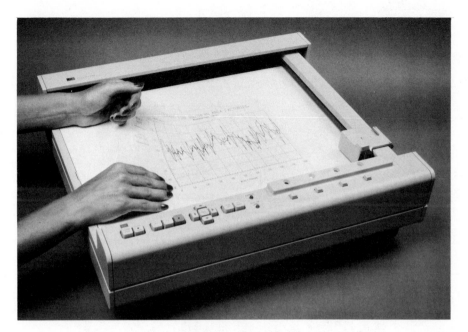

FIGURE 5-7 X-Y plotter.

used, as it is for laboratory data, there is, of course, no problem. This approach may be the only way to obtain high-speed plotting of rapidly changing data.

Illustrations of an *X-Y* plotter and a CRT plotter are shown, respectively, by Figs. 5-7 and 5-8. Characteristics of commercial printers, commercial CRTs, and commercial plotters are listed in Tables 5-1, 5-2, and 5-3, respectively. Table 5-3 lists just a few of the wide, ever-increasing variety of plotters.

5-6 CONTROL PANELS

Control panels appear in virtually all conceivable systems. A familiar example is the control panel of an automobile, which contains various control displays. There are switches to turn on lights, trouble-light indicators to warn of engine overheating, loss of generator power, or loss of oil pressure. There are also meters to indicate speed, to record mileage traveled, and to indicate the amount of gasoline in your tank.

In general, there are control panels associated with almost any equipment. Some have a wide variety of switches; some of the simple ones turn off or on a single circuit. Others select one of several circuits and are known as *multiposition switches*.

In addition to meters, switches, counters, etc., there are alpha-numeric displays. In a more complex system there may be a keyboard,

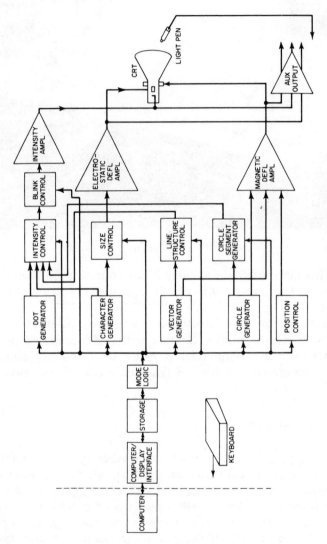

FIGURE 5-8 CRT mechanization.

TABLE 5-1

CHARACTERISTICS OF PRINTERS

Manufacturer	Integral Data	Tally	Lear-Siegler	Facit	C. Itoh	Data Products
Model	440	1200	300	4555	800	T-80
96 ASC II char. set	Yes	Option	Yes	No	Yes	Yes
Selectable characters	Yes	—	No	Yes	Yes	Yes
Lines/min	42	40	7 bidirectional	—	84 bidirectional	1500
Chars./line	132	130	136	130	80	80
Weight	20 lb		50 lb	55 lb	7 lb	22 lb
Dimensions	16W×12.3H×12.5D"	27W×17D×8H"	19W×7.5H×18.5D"			7H×14.7W×16.9D"
Power	—	—	160 W	150 W	—	—
CRT screen buffer	Option	No	Yes	No	No	Option
Parallel and RS232C interface	Yes	No	RS232C only	Yes	—	Yes
Matrix	7×7 or 8×7		9×7 or 9×9	7×5	5×7 options 7×7 or 9×7	5×7
Remarks	Mechanical print	Primarily used as terminal	Clock rates 75-9600 baud			This head prints by heat (thermal)

*All of the above devices are mechanical printers, where a matrix character strikes a ribbon.

TABLE 5-1 (cont.)

CHARACTERISTICS OF PRINTERS

Manufacturer	Datel	Florida Data	Perkins-Elmer	Data Printer	Qakadata
Model	AIP-40	PB-600	Carasell 350	3600	22
Print method	5×7 matrix	7×3 matrix	Print cup	Chain	5×7 or 7×9 impact matrix
Letters/line	40	130	132	132	132
Lines/in.	5	6	6	6	6 or 8 (operator selects)
Lines/sec	1.5	3.8	0.33	10	2
Marking method	Thermal	Mechanical	Print ball and ribbon	Mechanical	Mechanical (22 pin matrix) Each char. in series
Buffer	40 each	896	1 char. store	Each char.	Oscillating matrix. 4 passes to print 6 chars.
Print mechanism	All parallel	All parallel	Print ball and ribbon (serial)	Ribbon	
Code	Option: ASC II or RS232C	Option: ASC II or RS232C	Option: ASC II or RS232C	Option: ASC II, RS232C, or EBCDIC	ASC II (12 fonts on command)
Size	9H×15D×19W" (approx.)	10H×26D×24W"	9H×24D×28W"	40H×19D×27W" (approx.)	8½H×22D×23W"
Weight	15 lb (approx.)	70 lb	75 lb	250 lb (approx.)	85 lb
Power	—	700 W	—	800 W	360 W
Remarks	8-bit parity or RS232C interface	Can do graphs or columns	—	Forms length selection; parity check; 96 or 128 char. set; operator selects 10 lines/in.; paper motion detector	RS232C interface normal but can have 8-bit microprocessor interface (parallel); form width selector (3 to 14 in.) 12 in./sec paper flow rate

TABLE 5-2
CRT CHARACTERISTICS

Manufacturer	DEC	Hazeltine	DEC	Datamedia	Ann Arbor Terminals	Applied Digital Data Systems
Model	VT1CO	1552	VT52	DT80/1	VI52 Comp.	Regent 100 VT
Screen size	6.75×9.87"	6×9"	12×12"	5×9"	15" diag.	12" diag.
Reverse video	Yes	Yes	No	Yes	Option	Yes
Line/insert	Option	Yes	No	Yes	No	No
Special keys	Setup scroll	3 std.	3 std.	Setup scroll	26 optional	3 std.
RS232C interface	Yes	Yes	Yes	Yes	Yes	Yes
Self-test	Yes	No	No	Yes	Yes	Yes
Speed (baud)	50–19K	110–9.6K	75–9.6K	50–9.6K	110–9.6K	74–9.6K
Graphics	Yes	Yes	Yes	Yes	Yes	Yes
Rows/columns	24–80, 10–132, 24–132	24–80	24–80	24–80, 14–132, 24–132	24–80	24–80
Symbol size	7×9	7×10	7×7	7×9	7×7	8×8
Remarks	matrix Advanced video option; current loop (90 day guarantee); under-lining (option)	matrix VT-52 keyboard Alt. keypad; hold screen mode; typamatic keyboard	matrix No longer in production	matrix Video option; current loop; underlining	matrix First to supply reverse video	matrix Terminal bypass printing; alternate keypad and hold mode screen

TABLE 5-3

PLOTTER CHARACTERISTICS

Manufacturer	HP[a]	HP[a]	Gould	Versatec	Honeywell (dual unit)
Model	7225A	7047A	5005	2030	TM-80
Platform surface	Flat, $8\frac{1}{2} \times 11"$	Flat, $10 \times 15"$	Up to 11" wide	28.6" wide	—
Drive	Digital servo	Analog servo	Roll	Roll	Roll
Plotting speed (in./sec)	3 each axis	76 each axis	8.9	7.6	180
Chars./sec	3	—	64-128/sec	—	—
Size	$5\frac{1}{2}HX15DX16\frac{1}{2}W"$	$7HX17\frac{1}{2}DX19W"$	$7HX21DX28\frac{1}{2}W"$	—	—
Control	Digital counter servo	Servo; type not specified	Staggered stylus	Parallel stylus	Staggered stylus
Weight (lb)	17	41	—	—	—
Power (W)	70	180	—	—	280
Printing method	Inked pen	Inked pen	Electrostatic	Electrostatic	Thermal
Dots (if used)	—	—	100/in.	100/in.	70/in.
Type	X-Y	X-Y	Roll	Roll	Roll
Remarks	—	X: 3000 in./sec; Y: 2000 in./sec	Printer/plotter	Printer/plotter; all possible interfaces. TTL level. RS232C for CRT	5×7 matrix for printing

[a]Note: The abbreviation HP stands for Hewlett-Packard, Inc.

CRT, printer, plotter, or some other device. For example, consider the main display panel for a power plant. Such a panel would contain a series of display lights, called *annunciators*, which indicate to an operator any of a number of unusual conditions. The operator can then actuate the controls necessary to restore normal conditions, sometimes with the assistance of a computer. Such instrumentation provides for automatic power monitoring and control. A general discussion of a computer-controlled power plant appears in Chapter 8.

5-7 ALPHANUMERIC DISPLAYS WITH EMPHASIS ON NUMERICS

One kind of useful panel display is a lighted alphanumeric display. During the 1950s it was customary to display only decimal digits via decimal counters or devices called *nixie*, or *decatron, tubes*. These were all vacuum tube driven, using 50 to 400 V, hardly suitable for 5 V logic. These first displays were numeric only. Now there are a variety of display methods that employ several techniques. Alphanumerics can be displayed by 5 × 7 dots or larger dot matrixes, as indicated for printers and CRTs. Numerics alone, and some letters, can be projected from seven-segment light-emitting diode devices (LEDs). Seven-segment LEDs cannot display letters such as *M, V, Z, W*, etc., but they are convenient for displaying numbers and in fact the entire HD code. Figure 5-9 shows an LED numeric display device. This device can be actuated by the HD code, and the code can be stored and converted to seven-segment displays by special logic networks. A diagram of a system accepting numbers in series, storing each one, and driving a BCD-LED converter is shown in Fig. 5-10. BCD numbers in sequence are input and stored in successive latches.

The individual LED segments light when the transistor base goes

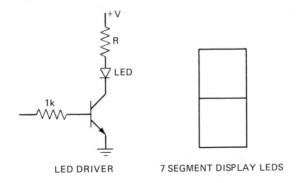

LED DRIVER   7 SEGMENT DISPLAY LEDS

FIGURE 5-9 HD-LED displays, using 7 segments.

positive. The amount of current through the resistor, transistor, LED circuit is controlled at a safe value by the resistor. BCD data and five alphanumerics may be coded and displayed. The simple driver is shown in Fig. 5-9. A number of digits may be multiplexed by the decoder, the segment drivers, and the digit-select drivers of the figure. Each digit is latched so as to continue to glow. Thus, the display remains visible until updated by a new load.

Other alphanumeric display systems do not employ matrixes or LEDs. Liquid crystal displays are now being marketed. When variable displays are not required (for example, warning indicators on a power plant panel) then simple, lighted annunciator displays, labeled only with their function, can be used. These are not sophisticated devices; having been used for many years, their use function is familiar to personnel.

Other kinds of displays for alphanumerics besides seven-segment LEDs and CRTs now exist. Matrix displays of 5×7, 8×7, or 9×7 dot matrixes are now used frequently. These can display the entire EBCDIC or ASC II codes; thus, the limitation to numerics only is avoided (formerly, seven-segment displays were essentially limited to numerics). In Fig. 5-11 we show a display loaded from a RAM memory, where the

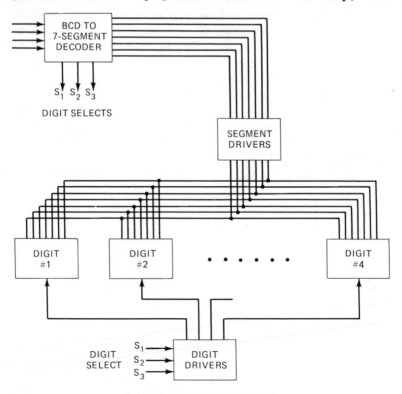

FIGURE 5-10 Multiplexed LEDs.

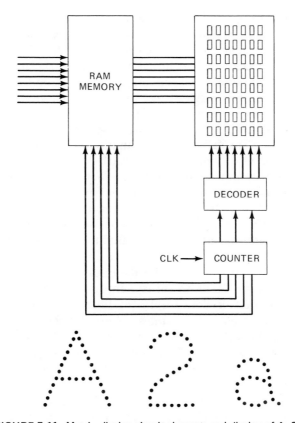

FIGURE 5-11 Matrix display circuit elements and display of A, 2, and a.

characters displayed were previously stored. The RAM-stored bits are sent over directly but are sequenced in succession by the counter; this occurs so quickly as to be indiscernible: this decoding process is not apparent to the eye; one sees only a flickerless display. If this is a CRT display the beam advances one character width, and the process is repeated for the next character in the sequence. The same process applies if the next character is in a crystal matrix display. The entire process for a display of several characters is on the order of milliseconds, so the entire display, even if it completely covers a scope, is virtually flickerless and easily readable.

5-8 HEADS-UP DISPLAY EXAMPLE

An important type of display used in commercial and military aircraft is the so-called *heads-up display* (HUD). Information is projected directly on the windshield in front of the pilot, thus minimizing actual checking of the instrument panel. Such factors as heading, altitude, airspeed, groundspeed, and even location coordinates appear on the HUD. Even attitude (roll and bank angles), for example, can be displayed, so the pilot need not remove his or her view from the windshield. Normally, there are two processors. One gathers all the analog inputs from the altimeter, airspeed meter, and heading indicator and converts these to digital quantities for transmission over a digital link to a second computer, which operates the HUD display. The first computer samples the TACAN navigation system, altimeter, and any weapons data. It essentially takes in analog data and generates their digital equivalents, all of which are transmitted to the second computer for analysis. As a weapons computer, the first computer also reacts to some communication circuits which signal whether an approaching aircraft is friend or foe. In reality, to perform as a weapons computer, A/D, S/D, and other converters are used for the digital conversion function. Other inputs are from the flight computer—again all are analog.

A weapons computer and a heads-up-display computer can be interfaced by four UARTs (universal asynchronous receiver transmitters) if a command to transfer data on 16-bit lines from one to the other does not have to be greater than one-sixteenth of the computer clock. This approach is shown by the diagram of Fig. 5-12: to simplify the diagram only the main elements are shown. Normally, data travels in two groups of 8 bits between computer serial UARTs, which in turn divide the data bus (16-bits parallel). A bit-check mode is added, which blocks the serial transfer and instead transfers data from the output flow serially through the bit-check circuits, where the data appears a few microseconds later at the parallel input data bus. This data is then compared by software to verify that it matches the transmission, and then the bit-check is applied to either computer periodically. If there is doubt about serial transmission/reception, a serial message can be transferred through the serial path and checked by the other computer. The advantage of this method is that it uses a total of less than 12 components per side.

The UART accepts the 7 bits in parallel and outputs them in serial, along with the start bit, the data (7 bits), parity, and a stop bit. This is serial asynchronous transmission. The input is from the keyboard, and the output is to a serial line, that is, Teletype, for example. The clock to the UART is 16 times the baud rate at the output, which permits the fifth, sixth, or seventh clock to clock the data. For example, crystal oscillators at either end are not necessarily connected together; hence, each UART in a loop may have its own clock, not synchronized to any other.

Of course, the pilot and the control panel are also involved. There are some self-test buttons to press so as to check the system with simulated inputs, thus ensuring that the system is operational. Pressing

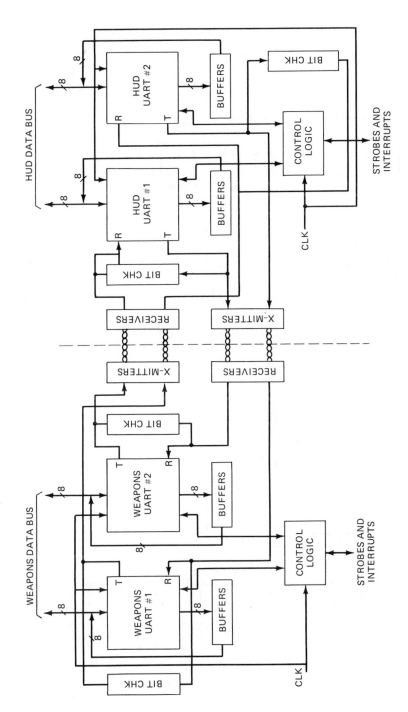

FIGURE 5-12 Dual UARTS for 16-bit transfers.

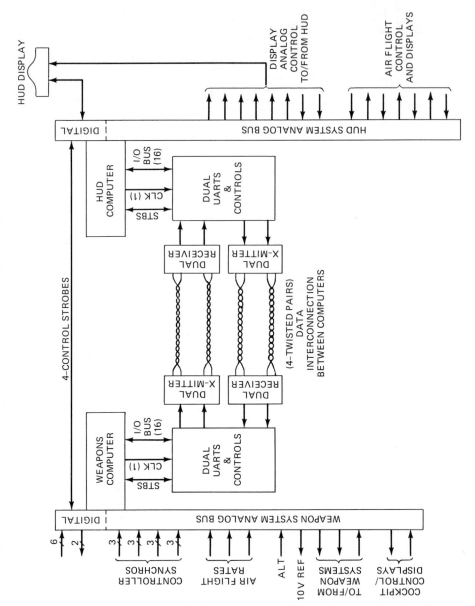

FIGURE 5-13 Weapons computer and heads-up display computer.

106

a test button produces a specific displacement of a dot on the HUD display. Thus, the system can be both self-checking and force-checked, depending on the pilot's preference. Longitude, latitude, and altitude are displayed as alphanumerics; roll, pitch, and heading can be displayed either as numerics or in animated form. Both computers exchange data via the system explained in the previous section, that is, via a serial bidirectional data link. Formerly, computer interfaces were completely analog, but rapid advances in digital technology convinced customers that the digital approach was the best way to go, especially considering the acceleration of microprocessor technology. The system must qualify to meet the most stringent of military specifications, since its reliability is of the utmost concern. Among such concerns are resistance to shock and operational vulnerability due to extreme variations in temperature during military operations. Figure 5-13 shows a complete weapons computer and heads-up display computer.

5-9 SUMMARY

In this chapter we outline display devices, including printers, CRTs, plotters, and numeric displays, and we conclude with a brief example of a highly accurate, complex, airborne computer system that has, in earlier versions, flown in several aircraft. The new system design is specifically for the Harrier aircraft of the U.S. Marine Corps, but seemingly is versatile enough for many future applications; this system is a joint effort of plants located in England and the United States.

The most important characteristic of displays is that of providing communication between a computer and a human being—the opposite

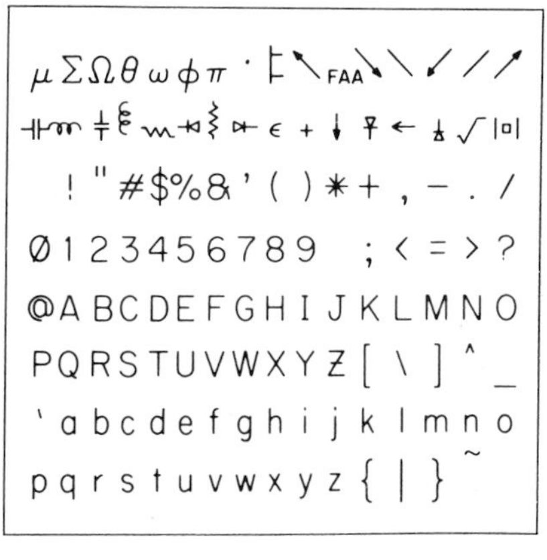

FIGURE 5-14 Symbols for character generation.

of loading devices in this respect. The lowering of costs of mini- and microprocessors has also accelerated the design of more competitive devices.

Since this chapter deals with the more sophisticated types of displays, we decided to include in Fig. 5-14 some symbols that are typically used with CRTs.

6

Computer Interfacing

6-1 INPUT/OUTPUT

The input/output section of the processor is normally the area of most concern to a system designer, because the I/O section is where the remainder of the system joins the processor. For a typical commercial system, the processor manufacturer provides logic to match the standard peripherals such as paper tape equipment, Teletypewriters, disk files, CRT displays. However, for many control systems, the devices the processor interfaces with are specially designed for a particular application, and peripheral control units (PCUs) are not always available as standard catalog items.

There has been progress in dealing with such special input/output requirements. Manufacturers have recognized that interfacing equipment does tend to fall into specific categories; hence, modules are available to interface specific types of signals or channels. These modules may be combined to handle multiple signals or channels of various types and, in a sense, provide a custom peripheral control unit. The overriding consideration, however, is that the data and control interface with the processor arithmetic unit and memory must be digital.

Thus, if the processor is to evaluate a number of dc voltage signals, the usual approach is to sample each such dc voltage signal and immediately to convert the voltage to a digital number equivalent. A device called an *analog-to-digital converter* performs this function nicely. Since dc voltage usually changes its level slowly (compared to the speed of the processor) and the converter will require less than 100 μsec to perform its function, many dc levels can be evaluated in, say, a second. Hence, a device called a *multiplexer* can switch in sequence a number of dc test points to a single analog-to-digital converter input. Therefore, two standard modules often available for central system interfacing are a multiplex switch with perhaps 4, 8, 16, etc., channels and an analog-to-digital converter. Depending on the system, more modules of the multiplex switch can be added as more channels are required. Similarly, multiplexers can be provided for multiple digital inputs, ac inputs, and special analog measuring devices such as synchros and resolvers.

For the opposite case, the processor may well be required to furnish outputs to analog equipment. Here the process of demultiplexing directing a single output to many devices is equally useful to multiplexing in the former case. Also, devices called *digital-to-analog* converters convert the digital processor output to analog voltage where necessary. Again, these interfacing units can be built up from grouped modules in most instances. Figure 6-1 illustrates a typical control processor input/output arrangement.

The Electronics Industry Association (EIA) Standard RS232C imposes standards for short-haul data transmission in serial form and defines the interfacing signals, equipment standards, and data rates. It is used to interface MODEMS. There are 25 lines specified, but only the most important are included in Table 6-1.

The following are the standard bit rates (baud) for RS232C.

19,200	*1,200*	*110*
9,600	*600*	*75*
4,800	*300*	*50*
2,400	*150*	

"Handshaking" modes are in effect for RS232C links; that is, one terminal states, "I have data ready." The other replies, "Send." It then says to the first terminal: "I have received successfully."

Because so much variety is to be expected for input/output requirements, the basic control processor is usually supplied with only a Teletypewriter, a control panel, or some other means for loading programs and recognizing that the processing is proceeding properly. The purchaser must elect what other peripherals are required and either design an interface for them or procure available standard units. Recognizing the fact that the design of special interfaces is sometimes necessary, processor manufacturers furnish complete definitions of their

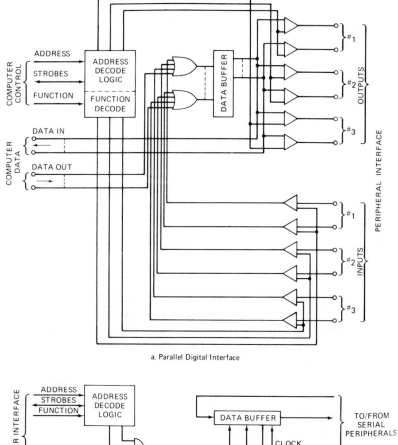

a. Parallel Digital Interface

b. Serial Digital Interface

FIGURE 6-1 A typical computer interface.

product's interface system and capabilities. These definitions usually include:

1. The number and types of channels available.

2. The number of bits available in the input and output data words for each channel.

3. The method of addressing peripheral devices.

4. The definition of strobes required to address, to transfer data, and to assure proper transfers have been achieved.

Table 6-1

SUMMARY OF EIA RS232C SIGNALS

Signal	Lines	To COM	From COM
Ground	1		
Transmit data	1	X	
Received data	1		X
Request to send	1	X	
Clear to send	1		X
Data set ready	1		X
Data terminal ready	1	X	
Ring indicator	1		X
Receiver line signal detect	1		X
Signal quality detect	1		X
Data rt. sel.	2	X	X
Transmit timing	2	X	X
Receiver timing	1		X
Seconding data and requests		X	X

5. Electrical restrictions, such as voltage ranges for valid "1s" or "0s", impedance restrictions on the interfacing equipment, maximum noise levels permitted, number of loads allowed, ground shifts allowed between equipment, data form, method of converting multiple inputs, etc.

6. Timing restrictions, including timing relationships between data and strobes, length of strobes, maximum speeds with data transfers, maximum and minimum rise and fall times of signals.

7. Physical restrictions such as length of cables permitted, type of connectors, type of lines, number of lines, and cables.

8. Any special interfaces such as direct analog lines, range of permissible voltages, impedence levels, accuracies.

9. Special provisions for devices interrupting the central processor. The numbers and characteristics of these will be specified.

10. Provisions for setting output discrete line signals or for accepting discrete signals for external equipment.

11. Provision for recognizing what equipment can generate the discretes or interrupts.

12. The maximum number of interrupts and discretes available or that can be added as options.

13. The methods of establishing an interrupt's priority and for masking out selected interrupts under program control.

14. Specifications of the input/output instructions available for operating the input/output system.

15. A description of timing clocks available from the processor or the timing signals the processor will accept.

16. Is the channel directly under program control or is it a "buffered" channel? If the latter, specification of the number of words that can be buffered, the range of memory that can be addressed by the buffer, the instructions available to test, set up, and control the channel.

6-2 BUSES AND FUNCTIONS

6-2.1 Serial Buses

Buses connecting the processor to other devices are of several classifications. First, there is the serial bus, which carries data 1 bit following the previous one in time sequence. This bus may consist of two single lines, usually shielded, carrying data in both directions, that is, outboard data on one line and inboard data on the other. Or another variation to reduce the effect of induced noise and interference can be accomplished with a twisted pair of wires that feed a differential receiver which, in effect, cancels the induced interference. Data can be straight binary or coded in Manchester form. There are, in addition, several control lines such as listed by the EIA Standard RS232C in Table 6-1. Also, it is quite usual to require a "handshaking" mode; that is, the computer says, "I am ready to ship data. Are your ready to receive?" If the answer from the other line is "yes," data is transmitted.

As described in Chapter 8 this interface has been recently revised to greatly increase data transfer rates in the serial mode.

6-2.2 Parallel Buses with Separate Input, Output, and Address Buses

This form of multiple bus is still popular and consists of three separate buses (input, output, and address) and a number of control lines. This type of bus (usually 8-bit bytes or 16-bit words) is usually of the "handshaking" mode type. Very often a PCU may signal to the processor the need to transfer data by raising a common interrupt line, or in more complex systems, each PCU may have its own interrupt line. This type of interrupt system is called a *vectored interrupt system*. The characteristics of a parallel bus system is shown in Fig. 6-2.

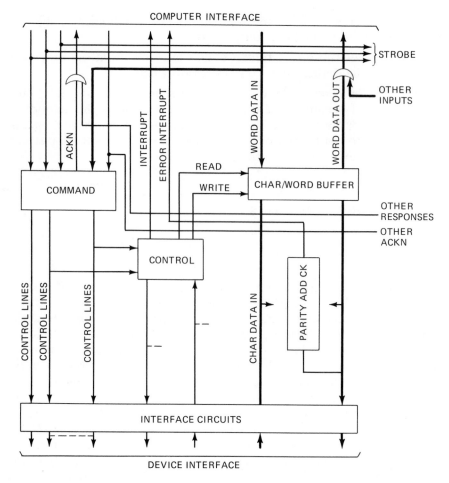

FIGURE 6-2 Generalized PCU block diagram.

6-2.3 Bidirectional Buses

In this form of bus 8 bits (byte) of data or 16-bit words of data going in either direction use the same wires. Usually, there is a unidirectional address bus and numerous strobes and control lines. Interrupts are also normally available. The address bus often addresses the main program ROM memory, the RAM memory, and the PCU interface elements as well. This bus form first appeared in fourth-generation minicomputers and then in virtually all of the microprocessor designs. Chapter 8 discusses in brief detail some of the present standard forms of these buses, but in this dynamic field today's standard is obsolete a year later.

6-2.4   Final Notes

In early systems and even at present both addresses and data are occasionally sent over the same set of lines outbound, with merely a strobe identifying whether the word is address or data. Another variation can be accomplished by having the PCU recognize the first transmission as address, followed immediately by a second transmission of data. An 8-bit (byte) bus is most common, since ASC II code requires 8 bits for transmission and many PCUs and peripherals are byte oriented. ASC II codes are used for serial transmission also, with start bits and stop bits added. This transmission form is asynchronous.

6-3   PERIPHERAL CONTROL UNITS

The general function of a peripheral control unit (PCU) is to provide the necessary interfacing between a peripheral device and the computer input/output. The PCU provides decoding of the computer commands relating specifically to a particular peripheral device; also, it develops the necessary control voltage levels, strobes, etc., as well as timing for operation of a peripheral device: for instance, a relay that stops or starts a device must be turned off or on. Applying power to the read or write amplifiers and selection of one of two speeds forward are a few examples of typical controls operated via the PCU. Other services rendered by the PCU may include:

- Conversion of the word format of the computer data to the character format for data in the peripheral device. If the peripheral device provides data input to the computer, the reverse conversion (character to word) may be called for.
- Provide circuitry to generate the proper drive voltages to supply output data lines and noise protection on input data lines.
- Provide special control signals and timing for its own internal operation during data manipulation and transfer.
- May provide, as an option, for the addition of a parity bit to outgoing computer data and check parity of incoming computer data.
- May have provisions for combining several incoming data channels into a single input channel before connection to the computer input bus.
- Can accept error indications from the peripheral device and

generate a computer interrupt advising the computer of an error.

- May be required in some instances to provide addressing control to a peripheral device.
- May be designed to control more than a single peripheral unit.

Although a portion of the electronics required to control a peripheral device furnished by the manufacturer, namely, that required to interface with a particular computer, is often neglected, this is understandable since peripheral manufacturers do not often know in advance who will purchase their equipment. Furthermore, computer interfacing requirements are generally nonstandard throughout the industry, although standardization is becoming an important consideration, especially for microcomputers.

A generalized diagram of a PCU is shown in Fig. 6-2. The two nominal methods of interfacing PCUs with computers is illustrated in Fig. 6-3.

The typical PCU receives its control commands from the direct I/O bus. In the simpler devices data flow in or out will be from the direct I/O bus also. Such devices as paper tape punches, paper tape readers, card punches, card readers, and slow-speed printers, incremental tapes, and keyboards would probably connect by this method. For the higher-speed devices control commands are still forwarded to the PCU via the direct I/O bus; bus data flow is via a buffered channel. This method, explained in the last chapter, permits data transfers without individual commands for each word transferred. Such peripheral devices as continuous-run magnetic tape, disk files, high-speed printers, CRTs, and plotters would probably use this approach.

In the block diagram of a basic PCU (Fig. 6-2), the function of the various sub-blocks may be briefly summarized in the following way:

> **Command decoder:** This subsection decodes the commands to the PCU and allows the PCU to generate control levels to the peripheral device, and sets the PCU in the mode to transfer data. It generates all the necessary control strobes to the computer or to the control device.

> **Character/word buffer:** This sub-block is required in some systems to sectionalize words of the computer into characters for the peripheral device. In the reverse transfer direction, the character/word buffer would assemble characters from the peripheral into a group and transfer this group into the computer as a single word. This mode of operation is called *packing*. Many systems do not require this buffer, since the peripheral and computer may both employ the same word length. The advantage to the computer

user's having such a device and using words is that the number of computer commands is reduced, since the transfer is on a word rather than on a character-to-character basis.

Control: This is the circuitry logic provided for the character/ word buffer to function automatically.

Interface circuits: This subsection includes all line drivers and input/output lines to/from peripherals, receiver circuits, noise rejection circuits, etc. Line drivers and line receivers are used to match the relatively low impedance of the lines to the high impedance driver circuits. They are often used to increase voltage levels or to convert the driving voltages to twisted-pair types. Receiver noise-rejection circuits will contain filters to remove unwanted line noise, although simple use of twisted-pair circuits is probably the best way to take care of this problem.

Parity check and generate circuits: Many peripheral devices have their own parity generation and/or parity check circuits, but this practice is by no means universal. Where there is a need for parity circuits and these are not provided in the peripheral, the PCU may be required to supply these functions where the devices themselves lack the capability.

Miscellaneous circuits: Many specialized functions may be included in a PCU if required. As an example, the PCU for a disk file will in most cases provide addressing registers for storage of address of data in the disk file. On other occasions it may be required to combine incoming data from several devices in the input bus. In this case a large OR gate on the computer input bus is likely. Such logic could well be part of the PCU.

Bidirectional buffers: With the advent of the microprocessor the major change has been to go to two-way data buses. The "handshaking" mode is still very much in evidence, but now many interface PCUs are single LSI digital integrated circuits, termed *DIP* for digital integrated package. Because the peripherals themselves still have one-way buses in many instances, the PCU's major function is to take bidirectional buses and convert these to the necessary one-way buses that were discussed previously.

There is a substantial list of features that should be specified, which makes it obvious why much thought and design can be expended during the process of connecting a digital processing system. For example, Fig. 6-2 depicts several features of a typical processor input/output section.

The physical connection problem is but one facet of interfacing.

One must consider carefully the impact of programming. Programs must be written to operate the peripherals, gather the input data when available, or send output data when generated. For the control system, multiplexers and demultiplexers must be addressed and the results of analog-digital conversions computed. All of this requires careful consideration to anticipate how often data will be transferred, from or to what channels, and in what order of priority. Thus, the input/output package requires a thorough understanding of hardware, software, and a system's requirements. Such understanding will help to provide an evaluation of potential features that will result in a final system that is both technically sound and economically feasible.

For standard peripheral devices, the manufacturer usually also develops the software for their operation. In some instances application programs are available for specific types of data-handling systems, and these can be employed, with only minor modifications, to new systems.

6-4   DIRECT INPUT/OUTPUT VERSUS BUFFERED INPUT/OUTPUT CHANNELS

6-4.1   Direct Input/Output (DIO)

Two basic methods are used to perform digital input/output word transfers; these are usually referred to *direct* or *buffered*. The direct (DIO) method requires the processor to execute one or more instructions for each word transferred either in or out. This scheme is economical of hardware but requires the separate instructions to share processing time with the other instructions that perform the computations. Thus, the inputting and outputting of data efficiently slows down the other processing steps. Nevertheless, an advantage of this system is that the input/output process is always under the control of the program.

6-4.2   Buffered Input/Output (BIO)

The BIO method allows the peripheral devices (or channel) to control the input/output word transfers. This removes some of the burden from the program or the processor, with the usual penalty of requiring additional hardware. However, the time the processor devotes to handling transfers (if they are between memory and the I/O channel) is lessened to the extent of one memory cycle for each transfer. This is faster than the DIO method, where each program transfer instruction usually requires at least two and sometimes three or four memory cycles to execute.

To provide BIO capability requires that the processor, via the DIO, load into special registers the following information:

1. The total number of words to be transferred.
2. The initial address in memory to (or from) which the transfer is to occur.
3. The direction of transfer.

Once this process is completed, the BIO channel takes over until the transfer process is complete, unless halted by a processor command or an error is detected by the BIO, which halts the operation. The memory is accessed only long enough (one cycle) to transfer the word. Figure 6-3 compares I/O control methods.

A diagram of a typical BIO channel is shown in Fig. 6-4. Here the peripheral signals its desire to transfer a word. The BIO in turn requests (via a strobe) use of the first available memory cycle. When the memory logic detects this strobe, it completes the program instruction it is presently executing and then raises a flag, which instructs the BIO to complete the transfer. The preset instruction counter (PIC), which was initially set to the address of the initial character transfer, is incremented by each transfer since the initial one and, therefore, contains a

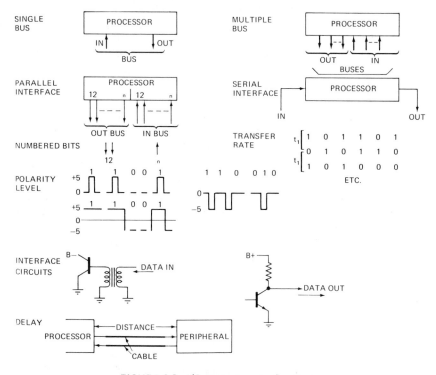

FIGURE 6-3 I/O channel control methods.

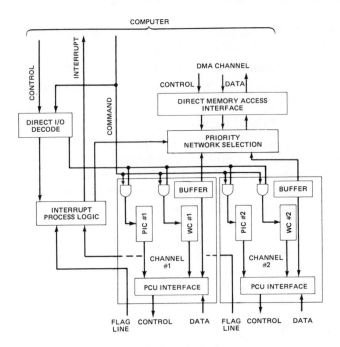

FIGURE 6-4 BIO block diagram.

memory address for the present transfer. In a like manner, for each word transfer the word counter (WC) is decremented. Provided the WC is not set to 0000 . . . , the transfer proceeds to (or from) the address specified by the PIC. When the WC is completely decremented, an interrupt is sent to the processor, closing off the present BIO transfer.

Because more than one BIO channel is often provided, and since the transfers are not controlled by the program, there is an excellent chance that two or more peripherals will demand a memory cycle at the same instance. To avoid conflicts that would create operational chaos, the multichannel BIO contains priority logic. This logic allows one channel to take precedence over others in cases of conflict. Usually, the individual channels are arranged in a priority sequence. A channel having a higher priority will prevail in any conflict, whereas one with a lower priority assignment will have to wait for the release of the channel by the priority selection logic before it can transfer data to or from its buffer. BIO is generally termed *direct memory access* (DMA).

6-5 EXTERNAL INTERRUPTS

Operation of DIO or BIO channels is enhanced by the use of external interrupts. Interrupts are "flag" lines that cause the processor to jump to a memory position which provides the starting address of a subroutine that services the indicated interrupt. Thus, a means is provided for both alerting the processor that a particular processing need presently exists, as well as a means for the orderly processing of that need. Once the interrupt is serviced, the "flag" line is reset, and the program jumps back to its normal routine.

Again, the need for establishing a priority exists. Should two interrupts occur simultaneously, obviously only one can be serviced at a given time. Therefore, the interrupt having the highest priority is serviced first, and those of lower established priority are then serviced according to their relative priorities.

Occasionally, processors have a means of blocking out interrupts selectively. This is accomplished usually by an interrupt blocking register which is loaded under instruction control. A bit on this register is assigned to each priority line. Provided a "1" exists on the bit assigned to a particular priority line, this line is in a non-blocked condition. Usually, internal interrupts are non-blockable and are assigned the highest priorities.

6-6 DISCRETES

Output discretes are individual lines outbound from a processor input/output to control such things as relays. These lines are controlled by the program and can be either logic signals or may have a power drive capability themselves.

Input discretes are individual signal lines inbound to the computer. They indicate that a specific condition exists externally, of which the processor should be aware. Input discretes differ from interrupts in that immediate service is not usually required. The program during its execution sequence will examine their setting periodically.

6-7 EXAMPLES OF TYPICAL PCUs

6-7.1 Computer-to-Computer Interface

Perhaps one of the more complex interfaces that occurs in modern systems is the connection of multiple processors—so they can communicate with one another. Such an arrangement is found in systems which employ remote processors to reduce data at the source and instead transmit it automatically to a centrally located processor. The distance between the processors can be hundreds of miles or the other extreme—just a few feet. The interface problem at the processors does not vary significantly whether or not there is a telephone link in between them.

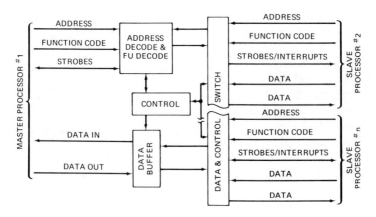

FIGURE 6-5 Computer/computer interface.

In general, since each processor operates asynchronously with its own clock, an intervening buffer must be employed in the data transfer path. Such an arrangement is featured in the block diagram of a processor/processor interface of Fig. 6-5. Here processor #1 is the "master"; that is, it initiates the control functions; and processor #2 is the "slave"—it responds to the commands of the "master." The method of operation is for processor #1 to transfer, under its normal command mode, data to or from the buffer register. The #2 processor then retrieves, by its own command mode, data from the buffer or provides data to the buffer for transfers in the direction of the "master." By employing interrupts or buffered channel control, the respective processors signal each other when the buffer is ready to continue the transfer, and also other status conditions.

6-7.2 A Printer PCU

Figure 6-6 shows a simple interface that is typical of a one-way transfer. The functions of each of the blocks has already been explained, so we shall not repeat that process. Basically, the transfer is outward from the computer; it would be the same for a tape punch, card punch, etc. Incoming PCUs are just as simple but often interrupt the computer to obtain its attention, so that it may jump to the subroutine which serves it. One system requires the printer to raise a strobe to signify that the PCU buffer is completely unloaded and is ready for the next character to be put in. The command logic opens the gates to the buffer. Depending on the code employed and if parity is included, these buffers can be made to hold from 6- to 9-bit codes. For a high-speed printer there often is a buffer for each column, which is parallel-loaded, and all must be loaded to print a line.

This is a very simple example of a buffer holding one character.

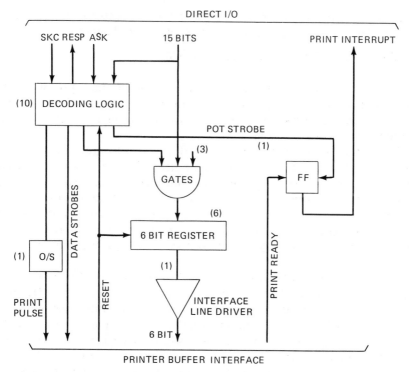

FIGURE 6-6 Printer PCU.

Quite often it is necessary to provide line-drivers at the computer end, especially if the computer and printer are some distance apart. There are many occasions when twisted-pair line-drivers and receivers are required at the two ends. This approach tends to eliminate the problems of noise interference and ground shifts.

To load a line in parallel we need a sufficient number of buffers to hold all characters; this often holds true for serial loading as well.

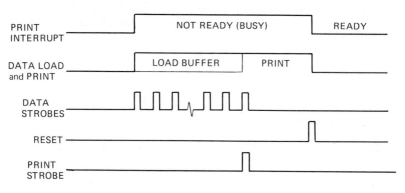

FIGURE 6-7 Printer PCU timing.

Figure 6-7 is a timing diagram: in this case the buffer is in the printer logic so that characters are loaded serially into the buffer.

6-7.3 A CMRT Typical Interface PCU

A typical PCU that would operate a magnetic tape system is illustrated by the diagram of Fig. 6-8. The list of controls is shown in Table 6-2. The timing diagram is Fig. 6-9. An approximate parts count by function is supplied by Table 6-3.

This PCU is the minimum required for a continuous-run tape unit. It is assumed that search operations in either forward, reverse, or bidirectional modes are accomplished by computer programming alone. In actual practice a search would be based on the addition of storage register hardware, which would hold for comparison a word or character. In some PCU designs that is done, but for the one proposed here this latter approach seems to go beyond the minimum design necessary for unit operation.

The data interface shown in Fig. 6-8 is via a buffered I/O unit. The use of a buffered I/O unit makes sense when considering the characteristics of a continuous-run tape. First, it permits transferring of groups of words with a minimum number of commands. Second, the program no longer needs to time precisely the interjection of the transfer commands into the program. Because computer word transfer rates must be aligned closely to the magnetic tape unit's character transfer rate, if a buffered channel is employed, it will ease the problem of tying together via a program two asynchronous devices.

6-7.4 Disk File PCU

The PCU for a disk file is somewhat more extensive than the one previously outlined for continuous-run magnetic tape equipment. The functions provided by the disk file PCU include the usual instruction decoding, data buffering, and interface match expected of all PCUs, but in addition, it must provide for addressing the tracks and sectors on the disk itself. One approach is to provide the address of the first sector and track from which to start and to allow the buffered channel itself to stop the transfer when the allotted words have been transferred. This arrangement works well when the transfer is of several words duration.

Normally, the selection matrix and switches for the original track heads (assuming head/track organization) are included with the disk file. When this is the case, the PCU must supply a head address and that address is stored either in the device or the PCU for the duration of the transfer. The address of the sector is also stored in a separate register, and for the purpose of explanation we shall assume that particular register is in the PCU.

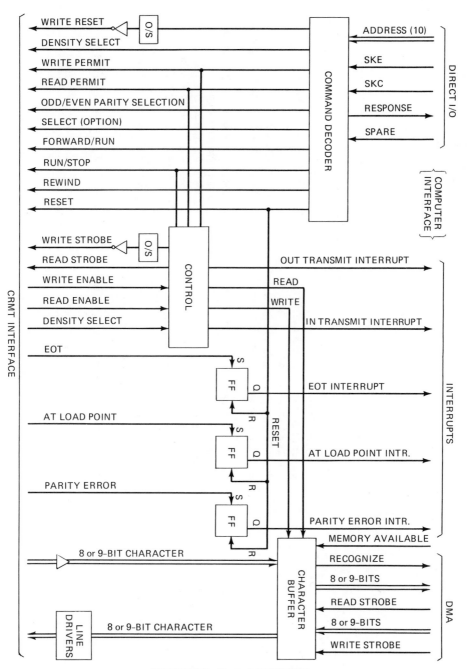

FIGURE 6-8 Typical CRMT PCU.

TABLE 6-2

LIST OF CONTROLS FOR CONTINUOUS-RUN MAGNETIC TAPE

A. Input Controls and Signals	Function	Interface
1. Write data	Data to be recorded. This is a level logic. 7 lines	0 V or −4.5 V during data interval, −4.5 V true
2. Write strobe	Negative going strobe. 0.8 μsec after edge of data interval	Pulse, 1–3 μsec. 0 to −4.5 V
3. Write reset	Write longitudinal parity check character	Pulse, 1–3 μsec. 0 to −3.5 V
4. Density select	In the true position selects high-density recording	Level, −4.5 V true and 0 V false
5. Write permit	Permits writing when write enable ring is in place	Level, −4.5 V true. Only applied when tape has stopped
6. Read permit	Permits reading	Level, −4.5 V true, 0 V false
7. Odd/even parity	Selects odd parity when true	Level, −4.5 V true, 0 V false
8. Select	Selects particular unit and puts it in ready status	Level, −4.5 V true, 0 V false
9. Forward/reverse	Selects forward direction when true and reverse direction when false. Must be set 1 sec before run/stop	Level, −4.5 V true, 0 V false
10. Run/stop	Causes unit to run when true and stop when false	Level, −4.5 V true, 0 V false
11. Rewind	Causes unit to rewind when true	Level, −3.5 V true, 0 V false

Table 6-2 (Cont.)

B. Output Signals and Alarms	Function	Interface
1. Read data	Data read from the tape. 7-9 lines	0 V true, > +2.5 V false
2. Read clock	A clock simultaneous with data on read data lines. About one-half normal data interval duration	0 V true, > +2.5 V false
3. Read parity error	A pulse is provided simultaneously with read data when parity check fails	0 V true, > +2.5 V false
4. Ready	Indicates transport is in remote state and ready	Level, 0 V false, > +3 V true
5. End of tape	Senses end of tape tab	Level, 0 V true, > +2.5 V false
6. At load point	Senses beginning of tape	Level, 0 V true, > +2.5 V false
7. Rewinding	Senses the unit is rewinding	Level, 0 V true, > +2.5 V false
8. Density select	Senses high-density selected	Level, 0 V true, > +2.5 V false
9. Write enable	Senses write-enable ring in place	Level, 0 V true, > +2.5 V false

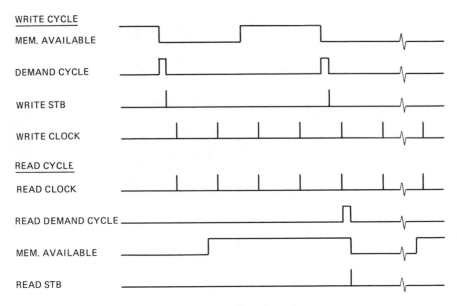

WRITE CYCLE

MEM. AVAILABLE

DEMAND CYCLE

WRITE STB

WRITE CLOCK

READ CYCLE

READ CLOCK

READ DEMAND CYCLE

MEM. AVAILABLE

READ STB

FIGURE 6-9 Continuous-read tape PCU data transfer timing.

The normal way for a transfer to begin is for the processor to place in the disk address registers an instruction word which contains the track address, the sector address, and a single bit to indicate the transfer direction (on or off the disk). The head can be selected immediately, but data may not be transferred until the sector and the proper head position are attained. To locate the proper sector, one technique is to employ a counter which is reset once a disk revolves past a sector mark. This index mark identifies the *first* sector, sector 1. As the disk spins, a new sector mark is detected as each sector passes. These sector marks are totaled in the counter. The counter contents, therefore, is a *record of the actual position of the disk*, to the nearest sector. When the sector count matches the address in the sector address register, the logic is arranged so that at the beginning of the next sector (at the sector mark) the transfer begins. The reader should note that the address for the transfer sector is in reality the address of the sector immediately preceding the desired sector.

If the data transfer of the disk is serial and the interface of the processor parallel, as is often the case, then an obvious necessity is to perform parallel/serial conversions when outputting from the processor and serial/parallel conversions when inputting to the processor. This general process is often accomplished by a two-level register-one level's being a serializer and the second level a buffer. This approach permits the data stream to and from the disk to be nearly continuous. If a 16-bit word is transferred between the processor and the buffer, and this

Table 6-3
CONTINUOUS-RUN TAPE PCU PARTS COUNT

Function	4 Each Dual Input NANDs	2 Each Four Input NANDs	1 Each Eight Input NANDs	FF	O/S	Power Drivers	Dual EX-OR	Misc	Function Total
Command decode	6	5	2	10	2	5			30
Control	6			7	4				17
Character/word buffer	20	18		16		2			56
Interface						15			15
Miscellaneous	1			3	2	2			8
Total	33	23	2	36	8	24			126

is to be accomplished as a parallel transfer, the words in and out of the
serializer should be 16-bit times plus 1- or 2-bit times properly allotted
to transfer between serializer and buffers. The parallel transfer here
occurs in one of the extra bit times mentioned in the previous sentence.
Therefore, a 16-bit word on the disk is 16 bits plus 2 bit positions not
used. The transfer between the buffer and the processor occurs at the
processor's convenience (as long as the convenience period is no longer
than the time required to serialize the second word). In other words,
during the serialization of a word, the previous word serialized waits in

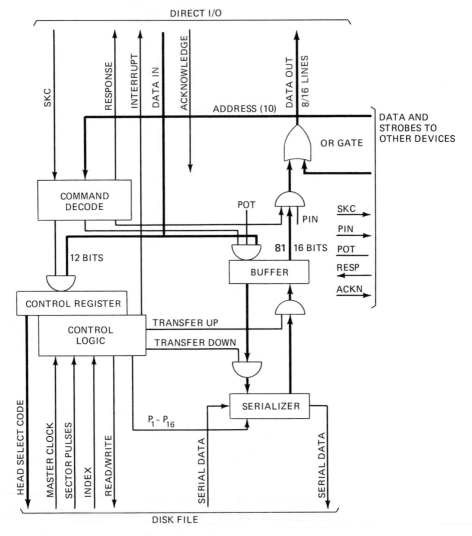

FIGURE 6-10 Disk file PCU block diagram.

the buffer for transfer to the processor if the date flow is to the processor. If the data flow is from the processor, the word transferred from the processor memory waits in the buffer until the previous word clears from the serializer onto the disk.

The logic for the PCU, shown in Fig. 6-10, includes a decoder section which starts, stops, and tests the disk's operating condition. The decoder also transfers the instruction address word into the disk address register, where it is held. The buffer and serializer as just described is, of course, a major part of the logic. The control logic for the PCU involves those elements that time and control the process. Since the disk file normally operates asynchronously with the processor, the control timing will normally come from the disk file itself. As a result the timing pulses to serialize ($P_1 - P_{16}$) and the buffer transfer pulse, P_{17}, are all derived by counting down bit-internal clock pulses from a track on the disk. This counter, the logic for recognizing a sector match, and the logic to allow the data transfer to start and end at the proper points, all are included in the control block. The interface matching circuits, as required, will be also a part of the PCU, and these are also indicated in Fig. 6-10.

Table 6-4 includes an estimate of the parts complexity of the disk file PCU. This list allows the reader to compare the relative complexities of the four PCUs described in this chapter.

Although nothing has been proposed so far for adding or checking parity, that check could easily be incorporated into the system. In a serial process, as the data transfers on and off the disk, the parity bit can be added as in any serial transfer by setting a flip-flop whenever a "1" is transferred. The read process for parity is merely to count the "1s" and check this against the flip-flop which stores a "1" or "0" parity flip-flop setting.

6-8 ANALOG AND DIGITAL INTERFACING

6-8.1 General

In this section we discuss the general characteristics of interfaces employed for real-time systems, that is, systems which are not controlled specifically by human intervention. Most peripheral devices considered up to this point have been entirely digital in their interface, either parallel or serial. A serial interface, that of RS232C, has already been covered. Character parallel transfers usually consist of 8 bits dumped into a character buffer register. In many of the newer interfaces these registers can be used for transfers in both directions. Presently, 16-bit transfers are more common, or two characters at a time.

Table 6-4

DISK-FILE PCU: APPROXIMATE PARTS COUNT

Function	Quad Inp.	2-NAND	Dual Inp.	4-NAND	8-Inp. NAND	Flip-flop	One-shot	Dual Power NAND	Dual EX-OR	Misc.	Total Function
Command decode	5		5		2	4	2	2			20
Control logic	14		29		8	17	4	2		3	77
Buffer/ serializer	8		1			48			48		105
Interface								52			52
Total	27		35		10	69	6	56	48	3	254

If there is more than a single peripheral, the OR function must be provided by this buffer. For multiple inputs to the computer, AND gates in the desired PCU are strobed. On outputs from the computer, the particular PCU is addressed to which the transfer is to occur.

In processing serial data, a serial shift register replaces the parallel character buffer. Another device mentioned in Chapter 1 is the universal asynchronous receiver/transmitter (UART). In either case the shift register or UART is shared for both transmission and receiving serial data.

We mentioned buffer registers one character wide; as pointed out, this case is not universal. Many computers have parallel buses from 12- to 32-bits wide, which generally is dependent on the computer's word length. A 16-bit bus is now very common for both minicomputers and microcomputers. In some cases address lines and the stobes as well as interrupts have their own lines.

6-8.2 Multiplexing

The multiplexing process involves the selection of an individual input line from several possible lines and connection of that line to a common point for as long as the selection logic permits. During another interval, a different line is selected and the connection to a common point performed for the new line—the first being disconnected, of course. The control for the selection is accomplished by sequencing logic that may have a predetermined selection routine, or it may be programmable via a digital processor. Multiplexers are considered to be *concentraters* of data and in the past have been called *commutators*; the latter term is more properly applied to the mechanical rotational form of switch used extensively in telemetry applications.

Figure 6-11 illustrates both a multiplexer and a demultiplexer.

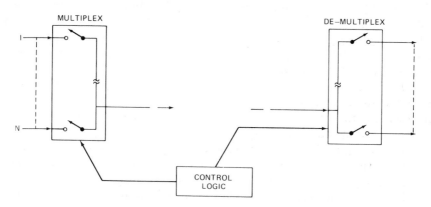

FIGURE 6-11 Multiplexing and demultiplexing process.

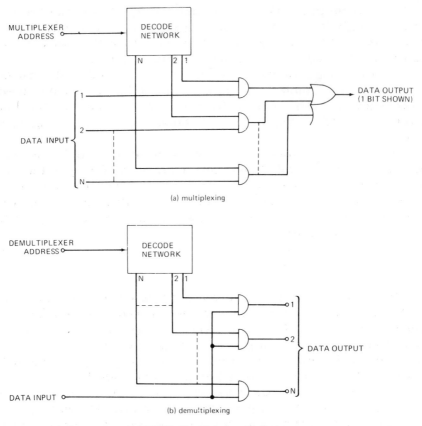

FIGURE 6-12 Digital multiplexing.

Demultiplexing is the reverse process (to multiplexing) of selecting one of several lines branching from a common point. The modern MOS-FET switching device can be employed effectively in both multiplexing and demultiplexing operations. This is possible since it switches in a bidirectional manner. As a result, the following sections treat the subject of multiplexing alone, but with the understanding that the material presented applies just as well to demultiplexing.

The discussion to follow concentrates on analog multiplexing, since the subject of digital multiplexing is well understood generally. In order not to completely ignore the digital classification, the following statement appears necessary.

Digital multiplexers are basically a concentration of AND gates, ORed together in the fashion illustrated by Fig. 6-12. If the data path is serial, a single AND gate for input data line is sufficient.

If the digital data is in parallel form, the gating must include the proper number of parallel paths. Digital multiplexing is generally to be preferred because the design of the gates is on a logic basis only.

6-8.3 Low-Level versus High-Level Analog Multiplexing

Analog multiplexing refers to the process of selecting and switching analog signals to a common junction point. If the analog signals to be processed are of millivolt amplitudes, the term *low-level multiplexing* applies. On the other hand, *high-level multiplexing* signifies that the multiplexing process is applied to signals of higher amplitudes, typically in the range of a volt or more. It is not unusual in an industrial multiplexing system to have it multiplexed first at low levels, followed by an analog amplifier; multiplexed again at a high level, followed by an analog-digital converter; and then the resulting digital signal multiplexed once more via a digital multiplexer before finally inputting the results to a digital processor. Figure 6-13 shows such a system in diagram form.

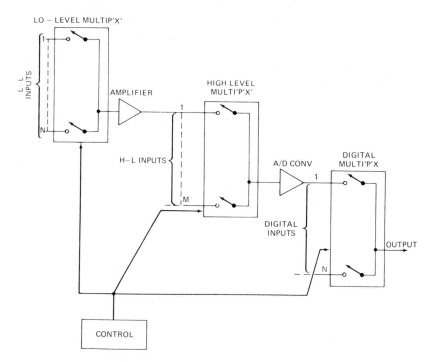

FIGURE 6-13 Typical multiplexer configuration.

6-8.4   Performance Factors

To describe the performance of a multiplexer, it is necessary to define several specifications commonly used. These specifications include scan rate, transfer accuracy, resolution, cross talk, and common mode rejection. The problem areas in multiplexer design revolve around cross talk and common mode rejection, as well as noise, resister imperfections, and offset drift. Switching time is often a problem, as is the isolation of signals from controlling circuits. A brief discussion of each of these factors follows.

Scan rate: The scan rate is deceptively simple. At first glance, it appears that scan rate is merely the number of channels divided by the time it takes to scan all channels. However, it is also necessary to determine that the scan rate thus arrived at is allowable in terms of the information frequencies contained in each channel. Theoretically, all data can be recovered if the sampling rate per channel is at least two times the maximum information frequency in the channel. However, in practical cases a ratio of 5 to 10 to 1 is more useful. From this consideration alone, a lower bound may be put on the allowable channel scan rate. The upper bound is the switching speeds of the multiplexer elements. In addition, aperture effects may also have to be considered, although that depends to some extent on what is done with the data after it leaves the multiplexer.

Transfer accuracy: Transfer accuracy concerns the relationship of the output data to the input data. It covers drifts, offsets, and nonlinearities in the individual channels. It should be noted that a specification for transfer accuracy should be commensurate with errors due to aperture and sample rate effects.

Resolution: Resolution refers to the ability to distinguish between adjacent signal levels, and it is a function of noise in the multiplexer.

Cross talk: Cross talk refers to signals from nonselected channels that may interfere with the selected channel reading. Cross talk arises in several ways. One type is due to the leakage resistance of the channel switches when off. Another type is due to the switch shunt capacities.

Common-mode rejection: Common-mode rejection, where applicable, refers to the ability of the multiplexer to separate differential signals on a two-terminal pair from signals applied equally to each terminal. Common-mode voltages pose a problem in that any unbalance in the differential input will turn the input into differential voltages indistinguishable from the signal being measured. Also, high common-mode voltages could break down the transistor junctions or otherwise damage the switching element.

Noise: Noise in multiplexers can come from several sources. A certain amount of noise is generated when a nonlinear operation such as switching occurs. This type of noise is unavoidable, and if it becomes a problem it can be eliminated by filtering. Another more serious source of noise is drive feedthrough from the control circuitry. Finally, the other significant source of noise is the amplifier that is often associated with multiplexers to buffer the output or input.

Resister imperfections: The resister imperfections in the switches allow currents from unselected channels to flow along with the selected signal. These leakages are a function of signal amplitude and temperature. The shunt capacities may store charge when a channel is amplified. This stored charge may then affect the reading of the next channel. Although this effect can be minimized by careful design, the shunt capacities also allow a certain amount of direct capacitive feedthrough. This factor often limits the number of channels in any multiplexer stage.

Offset: Offset is a function of the switch element. A well-designed element can have offset as low as 50 microvolts. What is more important is that, unless proper design techniques are used, the offset is temperature-sensitive. Over the temperature range required by military specifications, the offset might drift by many times its initial value unless proper precautions are taken.

Drift: To some extent, drift has already been discussed, but it should be noted that if an amplifier is used, then allowance must also be made for amplifier drift.

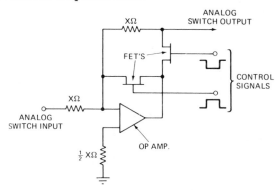

FIGURE 6-14 Precision analog multiplexer switch.

6-8.5   A/D and D/A Conversion Methods

The performance of analog-to-digital (A/D) and, conversely, digital-to-analog (D/A) conversions is fundamental to any hybrid analog/digital. The 2^nth step is compared to the remnant analog signal. If the analog signal is greater (but opposite in polarity), the logic allows the ladder step to remain applied and the 2^n register position logs a "1". This, in effect, subtracts a voltage of 2^n from the input signal. If the comparison shows 2^n to be too large, the present register bit is set to "0" and a subtraction of the 2^{n-1} voltage attempted instead. This sequencing continues through all n steps, and the eventual number stored in the register is the digital equivalent of the analog number. The magnitude of the input signal must be less than the sum of $\Sigma^n\, 2^n$ ladder steps of voltage to be within range of the converter. If both positive and negative polarity signals are to be converted, the reference voltage to the ladder network must be switched automatically by noting the original analog signal's polarity; an alternative solution would be to provide a compensating dc offset greater than the most negative voltage input to be handled.

For the D/A conversion process the digital number is stored as a register, which again controls the step setting of a ladder network. The

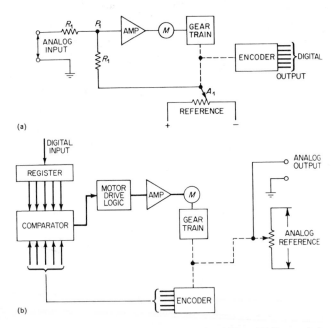

FIGURE 6-15   Electromechanical methods for A/D and D/A conversion.

output of the network via an operational amplifier is the analog output required. The operational amplifier serves to isolate the ladder network from the loading of following circuits. Both of the above processes are illustrated by Figs. 6-15(a) and 6-15(b).

Accuracy and response speeds of I-C forms of A/D and D/A converters is improving significantly. The key to this improvement cycle lies in the capability to build precise thick-film summing networks and switches that have uniform current-switching characteristics. Here each emitter carries approximately the same amount of current. Hence, to match circuits of similar characteristics should be an easier task than if each emitter carried a different current. An additional transistor is added to improve temperature tracking. The manufacturer, Analog Devices, Inc., claims that this approach leads to converters with accuracies of 14 bits plus sign. The response time using current-switching principles is reported to be 100 μsec for high accuracy, or a little more than 1 μsec for moderate accuracy.

If 12-bit accuracy is acceptable then the feasibility of putting the entire converter on a single chip (including the precision network) has been demonstrated. Hybrid Systems Corp. has announced their model DAC356 unit, which includes a thin film network deposited on the chip's oxide surface. This single 96 $\times$ 136 mil chip is reported to have most of the circuitry to provide 8-bit conversion. However, some of the supporting circuitry, including the operational output amplifier, is supplied by an additional flat-pac.

Synchro/digital and digital/synchro conversions are handled by the same general techniques, except that synchros are employed as the analog transducers.

Although electromechanical methods are accurate, they lead to relatively slow devices having appreciable moments of inertia. In addition, they are bulky, requiring a separate servo for each converter. They are also heavy and use a relatively large amount of electric power.

A completely electronic converter is obtained essentially by substituting electronic feedback for electromechanical feedback for the A/D case; a comparison is made at the input of a "comparator" circuit between the input analog signal and a composite feedback signal obtained from a linear, weighted-ladder network. The steps of the ladder network are controlled by a register which is stepped sequentially. Each step of the ladder generates a voltage which is one-half that of the preceding system. Consequently, the accomplishment of these processes is discussed first.

An electromechanical approach has been popular in the past. For the A/D conversion, an analog servo is often configured with a potentiometer feedback from the output shaft to the summing point at the amplifier input. The servo rotates whenever the analog input changes, the rotation being sufficient to advance the pot arm to the point where a balancing signal (therefore, the input amplifier is at null) is achieved. The output shaft also drives a shaft encoder, whose electrical output is a digitized representation of the shaft position and, consequently, is the converter's output. The process is illustrated by Fig. 6-15(a).

D/A conversions are performed electromechanically by a digital servo. In this case the digital signal to be converted to analog is generated again by positioning a shaft to which a dc pot, ac pot (vernastat), resolver, etc., are attached. The positioning of the shaft is obtained by comparing the digital number to be converted with the digital encoder attached to the servo's output shaft. The output shaft will rotate until a comparison is achieved; in other words, the shaft encoder will balance its output number to equal the digital number to be converted. This entire process positions the output shaft proportionally to the original digital number, as illustrated by Fig. 6-15(b). It follows, then, that an analog transducer added to the shaft will have as its output an analog signal proportioned to the original digital number. All electron D/A and A/D converters are shown in Fig. 6-16.

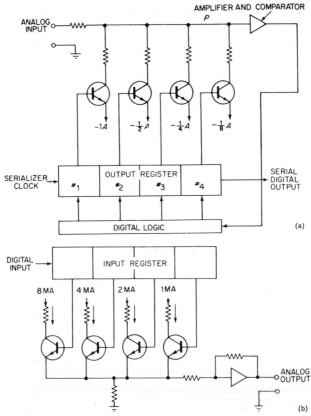

FIGURE 6-16 All-electronic conversion (A/D and D/A).

6-8.6 Synchro/Digital and Digital/Synchro Conversions

Synchros are a precision electromechanical device used to transmit a remote shaft position. The shaft's position, sensed by the transmitting synchro, is transmitted to a receiving synchro via three stator-connected lines. These lines are connected to windings having a spatial distribution of 120 degrees from each other. The voltages on the three lines are a modulated carrier. The relative amplitude and phase of the signals on the three lines defines the original position of the remote transmitter shaft to the receiving synchro.

Until recently, transmitter synchros communicated only with receiver synchros, as shown in Fig. 6-17. However, with the advent of the digital computer, there is a need to translate the transmitter-end shaft position directly to a digital word and input that word to the computer. A similar situation exists regarding the output of the computer; that is, it is necessary to now employ digital words to transmit shaft position data to a receiver synchro. The purpose of synchro/digital and digital/synchro conversions is to permit digital computers to be inserted in formerly all-analog systems, thus taking advantage of digital computers within the control system.

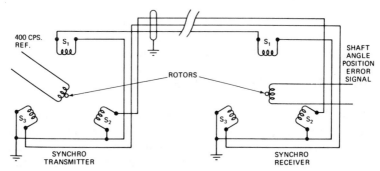

FIGURE 6-17 Synchro connectors.

6-8.7 Typical S/D and D/S Approach

A typical synchro/digital (S/D) converter is illustrated by Fig. 6-18. The three input stator lines are usually connected to the three-phase side of a Scott-T transformer whose output is two phase (two lines). The signals on these lines have values of $k \cos \theta \sin wt$ and $k \sin \theta \sin wt$, respectively, where θ is the position angle of the transmitter shaft and $\sin wt$ is the carrier. The carrier is normally removed by a demodulator which leaves the modulation terms ($k \cos \theta$ and $k \sin \theta$).

An ordinary analog/digital converter then converts the modulation terms to an equivalent digital number which, in turn, becomes an input to the computer. The computer may use the modulation terms directly to compute θ via:

$$\theta = \tan^{-1} \frac{k \sin \theta}{k \cos \theta} \quad \text{or} \quad \cos^{-1} \frac{k \cos \theta}{k \sin \theta}$$

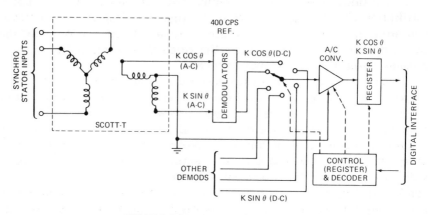

FIGURE 6-18 Typical S/D converter.

Figure 6-18 shows in block form a synchro/digital converter where the input is from a Scott-T transformer, and the output is the angle in linear degrees or radians, depending on how it is scaled.

6-8.8 Multiplexing and S/D and D/S Devices

Individual S/D and D/S converters for each synchro involved would be too expensive to be practical. As a result, multiplexing is usually employed to select one synchro at a time from many at the conversion system input. Separate A/D conversions are performed for the two demodulator lines of the selected synchro via the Scott-T transformer and the resulting $k \sin \theta$ and $k \sin \theta$ digital words obtained. The minimum rate at which each synchro channel is sampled depends on the expected upper limit of the modulation components. Typical sample rates would be 10 to 30 samples per second per synchro. Since the time per synchro sample (two lines) probably requires less than 0.5 millisec at 10 samples per second, 200 synchros could easily be serviced if, of course, the computer had nothing else to do.

Ideally, to reduce the number of Scott-T transformers involved in a system, multiplexing should be on the stator side. Although this is possible, the disadvantages are that the multiplexing switches must normally perform over the entire range of the ac waveform (about 11.8 V rms) unless attenuation of the signal is provided. To provide attenuation requires the addition of expensive components to the system. Therefore, it is quite common to multiplex after the Scott-T transformer, or even after the demodulator. If the multiplexing is placed after the demodulator, a single multiplexer can handle several dc signals for which A/D conversion is desired, as well as the synchros.

In a like manner, demultiplexing is employed for D/S outputs. In this case a sample-and-hold circuit is added on the synchro side of the demultiplexer to hold the dc level to the modulator between samples. The number of channels that can be time-shared is a function of the decrement error characteristics of the sample-and-hold circuit.

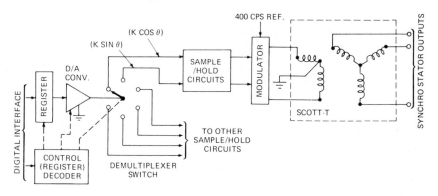

FIGURE 6-19 A D/S conversion method.

6-8.9 Attempts to Lower Cost (in Addition to Multiplexing)

For systems of the future, it would appear that completely solid-state (probably LSI) S/D and D/S converters are a desirable goal. The Scott-T transformer at present does not easily lend itself to LSI technology. Therefore, the question is can the Scott-T transformer be eliminated and what would be the cost of elimination? The cost is the addition of a line demodulator and the necessity of three conversions in place of two. (In this approach, all three of the stator voltages are evaluated.) Again, the cosine and sine terms of the θ position may be calculated from:

$$k \cos \theta = a_1$$

$$k \sin \theta = \frac{a_3 - a_2}{3}$$

where a_1, a_2, and a_3 are the three stator voltage amplitudes and polarities (a_1 is reference). Thus, the Scott-T transformer may be removed and completely solid-state S/D and D/S converters are possible, provided a computer is available for the computations of $k \sin \theta$. Where the tangent or cotangent is employed to calculate θ depends on where the shaft angle θ falls on the 360 degree circle. Generally, the tangent is not used in the vicinity of 90 degrees (or 270 degrees), since its value becomes equal to infinity (∞) here. A similar situation occurs for the cotangent near 0 degree and 180 degrees. Therefore, the S/D normally has segment sensing logic built in to detect the octant (45 degree sector) in which θ falls. Thus, knowing the octant , the tangent or cotangent computation can be selected as needed.

The D/S converter is the opposite of the S/D converter. Here digital words representing the $k \cos \theta$ and $k \sin \theta$ terms are converted to three-wire analog voltages properly modulating a $\sin wt$ carrier. The general approach is illustrated by Fig. 6-19 and includes two digital word registers, two D/A converters, two modulators, and a Scott-T transformer operating in a reverse direction to the S/D case.

6-8.10 When θ Is Desired at the S/D Converter Output

The angle θ in digital word form is easily obtained when a computer is available. However, the S/D device itself is sometimes required to output in digital form the angle θ directly. How is this accomplished? One of the typical methods is to employ trigonometric ladder networks in the A/D converter itself. A typical circuit employing a tangent network is shown in Fig. 6-20. Here the $k \cos \theta$ term is multi-

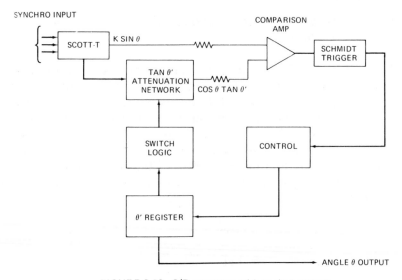

FIGURE 6-20 S/D converter with angle θ output.

plied by tan θ'. When $\theta' = \theta$, the two sin θ terms at the input to the computer are equal; therefore, the register setting controlling the tan θ' multiplexer must be set to θ. Again, the usual sectoring selections of the tangent and cotangent functions are necessary.

The primary disadvantage of the system is the need to employ expensive precision trigonometric networks (tangent, cotangent, sine, or cosine) that cannot be shared with the normal A/D conversions. In general, though, this approach may be less expensive than others.

Other approaches that could be considered would include a direct table lookup in a read-only associative memory. Here the sine θ or cos θ term entries would be the basis of a θ selection, of course, with the assistance of the sector logic. The problem then relates to the extensive logic required to select and read the contents of the memory, possibly a small processor in itself.

6-9 SUMMARY

This chapter treats the important subjects of input/output and computer interfacing in general. It begins by explaining a typical interface and some of the factors concerning them which a designer must consider carefully. The next section discusses different forms of busing, that is, lines where multiple connections are made. Section 6-3 defines a peripheral control unit (PCU) and discusses its organization in detail. Section 6-4 compares DIOs with BIOs. The BIO channel is usually referred to as *direct memory access*, or simply DMA. External interrupts are covered briefly in Section 6-5 and input discretes in Section 6-6. Section 6-7 explains the functioning of several typical PCUs, and Section 6-8 treats real-time processing devices such as multiplexers, D/A converters, A/D converters, synchro/digital and digital/synchro conversions. All these devices are used for interfacing with equipment not originally designed for digital systems (for example, aircraft instruments and machine tools).

7

Digital
Communications

7-1 INTRODUCTION

Because so much processor data is transmitted great distances, the communication channel carrying the data is important, since the communication link is an integral part of the processor system.

Originally, communication links were either voice, Teletype, or telegraph. Shortly before World War II, coaxial cables were first used to transmit wide-band television. Thus, transmission of video information of more than 4 MHz bandwidths was demonstrated. Also, the technique of frequency division multiplexing was perfected, thus accommodating hundreds of telephone messages simultaneously by a single coaxial cable.

Now data in binary serial form is also transmitted over the same or similar facilities. This additional workload has necessitated that telephone companies expand their vast facilities further for the purpose of transmitting binary data. Where waveform distortion caused only minor problems with voice transmission, similar distortion for high-speed data is unacceptable. Also, the telephone industry is already saddled with billions of dollars worth of voice transmission and switching equipment; therefore, economic considerations dictate the use of that equipment for data transmission as well, if it can be done. In this chapter we discuss how data transmission is accomplished with existing equipment and the compromises involved.

7-2 TELEPHONE AND TELEGRAPH SYSTEMS

Telephone and telegraph communications have been in use for many years in the United States; with the assistance of radio microwave links, scatter links, cables, and satellites, voice communication is now worldwide. Each voice subscriber is assigned to an exchange, and at that point local connections between subscribers are made and connections to and from other exchanges are made via trunks, if the call is to leave the local area. In order to handle the great volume of traffic the trend is to employ automatic switching of traffic at both the local level and for interconnecting of the exchanges. In addition, methods have been found to increase the capability of a single wire or channel to handle several messages at the same time. This combining of messages is called *multiplexing*, and without such a technique the vast worldwide communications complex would not be economical. The general approach is to connect many individual exchanges to a switching center and to then interconnect the switching centers in a nationwide hookup. At each higher switching level the multiplexing on each channel is increased; that is, trunks are multiplexed into groups, groups into supergroups, supergroups into mastergroups. Table 7-1 and Fig. 7-1

TABLE 7-1

TELEPHONE CHANNELS

A. *Multiplexed Channels:*
   1. *12 voice channels multiplexed together form a* group.
   2. *5* groups *multiplexed together form a* supergroup *(this is 60 voice channels)*
   3. *10* supergroups *multiplexed together form a* mastergroup *(this is 600 voice channels).*
B. *Important Definitions:*
   1. Channel: *A two-way communications path linking two suscribers.*
   2. Trunk: *A multichannel path between two switching centers. Usually, this is a two-way link.*
   3. Full-duplex: *A path that provides two-way transmission simultaneously.*
   4. Half-duplex: *A path that provides two-way transmission, but in only one direction at a time.*
   5. Dedicated line: *A communication path between two subscribers that is not switched. It is solely for connecting the two suscribers concerned.*

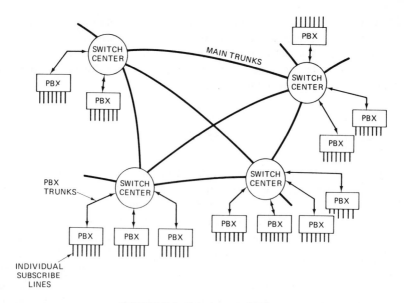

FIGURE 7-1 Telephone switching.

summarize this hierarchy on a general basis for this frequency-division multiplex network.

An individual telephone subscriber line is designed for the relatively narrow band of frequencies which carry voice intelligence. This band is approximately 100 to 3000 Hz. The bandwidth requirements at the group and supergroup levels increase correspondingly because of the increase in the amount of information to be transmitted. With wide bandwidths to be handled such transmission modes as microwave and cable become very attractive because many channels, as indicated by figures in Section 7-3, can be mixed on the single master carrier by frequency-division multiplex methods. Each voice channel is modulated with its own subcarrier, and the resulting modulation envelope occupies about 3 Hz, each channel being spaced sequentially within the total bandwidth allotted.

Telegraph or Teletype messages even require less bandwidth than voice; in fact, it is normal practice to frequency-division multiplex several Teletype transmissions on a single subscriber voice line. Just as for telephone, these lines in turn can be multiplexed into higher categories. Since normal Teletype transmission is primarily about 10 characters per second, with 8 to 11 bits comprising a character, depending on the code employed, upward of 16 to 20 Teletypes can be multiplexed on a single telephone subscriber line. This does not mean that Teletype equipment can be indiscriminately connected to a telephone line. In addition to using the proper multiplex couplers, precautions must be taken that the wave shapes of the Teletype pulses are within distortion limits; otherwise, transmission errors may occur. As a result telephone and telegraph lines are said to be *conditioned* for a particular class of service. Distortion is not considered detrimental to most telephone transmission, but it can be of serious concern in Teletype communications. Examples of typical Teletype codes are listed in Tables 3-1 and 3-2. Table 3-1 indicates the present digital code, although devices still operate (TTYs) in the code shown in Table 3-2.

For modern digital data traffic, the data bit form of transmission will be retained. There are, however, some differences to be noted over present Teletype transmission. For one, the data rates eventually will be much faster. Whereas a typical Teletype transmits at close to 100 levels per second (bits per second), the data transmission over telephone lines is 1200, 2400, or even 9600 bits/second. Under the latter condition, dedicated conditioned channels are most often used.

Teletype transmission can occur in either of two modes: asynchronous or synchronous. In the original asynchronous mode each character transmitted caused automatic synchronizing of the receiver. This synchronizing was achieved because an initial drop from a high to a low level signified the start of a character. The synchronous mode is used, however, where the multiplexing of several messages occur on a single line. In this case a clock is transmitted also from transmitter to receiver, in addition to the message bits. The clock synchronizes the receiver. Digital data transmission employs this method, especially where frequency-division multiplex is used. For synchronous transmission no start bit is employed for separate characters, but often an initial synchronizing code precedes the data transmitted.

7-3 VOICE CARRIER AND DATA MODULATION

The principal method of modulating a carrier with voice frequencies (100 to 3000 Hz) is to frequency modulate the carrier. The 100 to 3000 Hz audio signal causes the carrier to vary 100 to 3000 Hz above and below the carrier frequency. Thus, a 100 Hz carrier will have sideband frequencies of 999,900 and 1,000,100 Hz for a 100 Hz signal, and 997,000 and 1,003,000 Hz for a 3000 Hz audio signal. The extremes of this range are 997,000 to 1,003,000 Hz, which is defined as the bandwidth required to transmit the voice frequencies indicated on the carrier described. Figure 7-2 illustrates how frequency modulation places modulation bands on both sides of the carrier frequency.

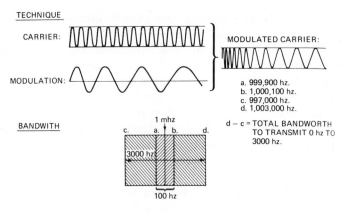

TECHNIQUE

CARRIER:

MODULATION:

MODULATED CARRIER:

a. 999,900 hz.
b. 1,000,100 hz.
c. 997,000 hz.
d. 1,003,000 hz.

BANDWITH

1 mhz

c.   a. | b.   d.

3000 hz

d – c = TOTAL BANDWORTH
TO TRANSMIT 0 hz TO
3000 hz.

100 hz

FIGURE 7-2 Frequency modulation.

7-4 FREQUENCY-DIVISION MULTIPLEX (FDM)

Multiplexing of voice channels is achieved by taking individual voice channels and adding each to a subcarrier that is spaced in frequency at greater intervals than the voice bandwidths; this process is shown by Fig. 7-3. Some additional spacing is required so that the voice channel modulations do not overlap to cause a noise condition called *cross talk* to occur. These subcarriers, and their individual voice modulations, are then allowed to modulate the main carrier. This series of modulated frequency bands thus appears transferred to and is transported by the main carrier. It is these bands that are separated by individual filters tuned to the respective subcarriers' bands at the receiving end. This process is called *frequency-division multiplex* (FDM).

Because digital data at 2400 bits/second can be carried by a voice channel, it too can be multiplexed on a main carrier in the same manner as voice. Therefore, a communication network can transport either data or voice—in some cases interchangeably. Care must be taken when transmitting data to avoid excessive distortion of the individual pulsed

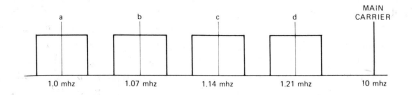

a   b   c   d   MAIN
                                                                          CARRIER

1.0 mhz   1.07 mhz   1.14 mhz   1.21 mhz   10 mhz

a, b, c, and d are Subcarriers Spaced in Frequency
Sufficiently to Transmit 0 to 3000 hz. Modulation.

FIGURE 7-3 Frequency-division multiplex.

signals; otherwise, excessive errors of interpretation can occur. Often, voice is intelligible despite great distortion, but data is extremely vulnerable to error under such conditions.

7-5 TIME-DIVISION MULTIPLEX (TDM)

A second form of multiplexing is illustrated by Fig. 7-4. This method is called *time-division multiplexing*, because the individual messages are separated in time. The reader should note that the data is already in the form of a pulse train; therefore, this method is especially useful for data transmission.

In time-division multiplex, a time slot in the master frame is assigned to each message channel. This same time slot in succeeding master frames is assigned to the same channel. The commutation at both the transmitting and receiving ends is synchronized so that proper routing between terminals is maintained. Therefore, the individual

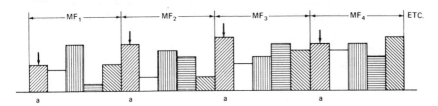

a. Time-slots Carrying Amplitude Samples

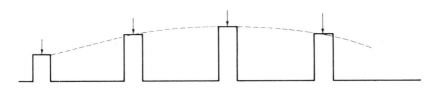

b. Example of the "a" Samples

c. The Required Multiple-demultiplex Arrangement

FIGURE 7-4 Time-division multiplex.

channel is subjected to bursts of pulses rather than a smooth flow of analog levels.

To achieve high data transmission rates with this system, it is necessary to use a high bit rate between commutations. Thus, from 1.04 MHz upward to hundreds of megahertz bit rates are predictable.

It is interesting to note that this system of multiplexing originated as a voice transmission system. In Fig. 7-5 the voice waveform is sampled, the level measured, and this latter measurement converted to a 7-bit binary code. These code samples are transmitted in a time-division multiplex manner to the receiving end. They are then de-commutated (converted) back to analog voice and then forwarded to the other subscriber. The Bell System's T-1 Carrier System can multiplex 24 telephone messages at 8000 samples per second, with an 8 bit per level sample. The eighth bit is a synchronizing bit. This system requires a carrier of 1.54 MHz. Development of much higher carriers is expected in the future, which will widen data-carrying capabilities correspondingly.

This system has no difficulty in transmitting data also, provided it is split up into the proper format to fit the constraints of the system.

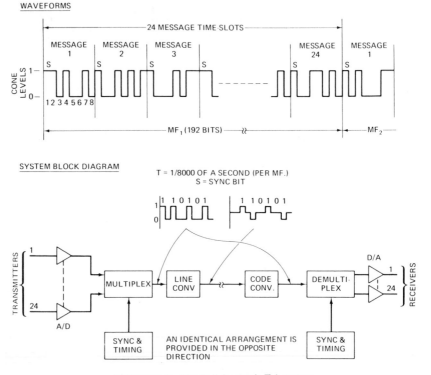

FIGURE 7-5 The Bell System's T-1 system.

The critical factor in TDM is maintaining total synchronization of the system.

7-6 HIGH-FREQUENCY (HF) RADIO

For long distance transmission of both voice and Teletype, high-frequency radio has been in use for a long time. However, it is not without its drawbacks, as anyone who has listened to shortwave radio can testify. In this transmission method, atmospheric conditions between transmitter and receiver can cause a wide variation in phrase, amplitude, and noise level of the received signal. These phenomena naturally are extremely annoying in Teletype transmission, and in fact, where radio is the primary path special methods are employed to transmit a message reliably. One such method is to limit the bandwidth and to apply more power to a fewer number of channels. That, of course, lowers the total number of transmission channels available but provides greater reliability for those channels available for transmission. Since channel noise is the usual limiting factor, and this is proportional to bandwidth, the above practice is, in effect, raising the signal level with respect to channel noise. When the signal-to-noise ratio is improved, more bits are transmitted correctly—that is, a "1" is recognized at the receiver more often as a "1" than as a "0" and vice versa.

7-7 FREQUENCY-DIVISION MULTIPLEX
FOR RELIABILITY

An interesting example of digital data transfer occurs in a military system for data over long distances via VHF. The transfer bit rate is 2400 bits/second serial bit stream for the digital data, but the individual bits are transmitted for over 13 millisec each. At a bit rate of 13 millisec per bit, only 70 bits/second can be transmitted normally. How 2400 bits/second are sent over this channel is a fine example of how multiplexing helps to put more information on a channel, even though the path is VHF radio. Figure 7-6 summarizes the channel characteristics.

Every 2 bits in a 32-bit parallel word are assigned a separate frequency tone. Because the 2 bits can combine as 00, 10, 01, or 11, there are four possible combinations. By phase modulating the tone to one of four phase conditions, it will transmit the bit pair information. By this scheme then, 16 tones will identify the 32 bits. The tones now with the phase information added are subcarriers. These subcarriers modulate the main carrier, and the frequency multiplexed signal is transmitted. At the receiver end, the demodulator reseparates the

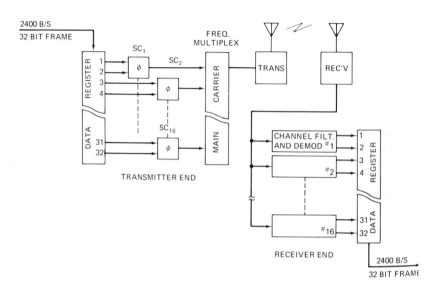

FIGURE 7-6 VHF transmission method.

tones, then phase information and the individual bit pairs are recovered in digital form. The advantage of this system is that had a single set of tones been used and the data forwarded as a serial bit stream, the tones allotted for each bit would have been only about 250 millisec long. Noise, fading, and other effects could disrupt a short tone more readily, and the individual bits could easily be lost or misinterpreted. By stretching out the time an individual bit is transmitted to about 13.0 millisec, the likelihood of misinterpreting the individual bits due to propagation medium abnormalities is lessened considerably. To put 16 tones on a single carrier, the carrier is frequency modulated by the separate tones. This composite signal (sidebands plus main carrier) is transmitted between sender and receiver terminals. At the receiver end, filters separate the 16 subcarriers plus their phase information, and the 32 digital bits are recovered by the demodulation process.

7-8 DATA TRANSMISSION BETWEEN PROCESSORS

Whereas Teletype equipment and models 28, 33, 35, and 37 are limited in their data transfer speeds because of their internal mechanical coding and encoding devices, digital processors can readily input and output data at megacycle bit rates. If two processors must communicate over a commercial telephone or telegraph path, the bandwidth capabilities of the path will be the limiting factor in the data transfer rate. As an example, telephone subscriber lines can easily transmit 2400 bits/second of binary data. With some of the newer facilities and newer forms of modulation techniques, the possible bit rates have been raised for a cycle to 4800 or 9600 bits/second, using modern MODEM equipment. Although this is considerably faster than two conventional Teletypes can communicate with each other, it is still much slower than the processors are capable of individually.

For other reasons also, a normal telephone network is not ideal for data transmission. Even at 2400 bits/second transmission rates, electrical noise (cross talk) and switching noise at the exchanges and switches can be too severe and thus cause errors during transmission. Therefore, at 2400 bits/second transfers, it is usually necessary at present to use dedicated lines. These lines are direct connections between two points and are not switched at the exchanges or switching centers. Of course, these lines cost a subscriber more to lease, but they improve the reliability of data transfer by cutting down on errors during transmission. Also, there are now several cities supplied by special switched wideband data paths, called *Dataphone 50*, which can readily carry 50,000 bits/second. This rate is more compatible with ideal processor data transfer rates; hence, processor link-ups appear now to be more practical from the communications standpoint.

7-9 MODULATION

As indicated previously, the form of data in a computer is typically at dc levels where 5 V equals a "1" and 0 V equals a "0". In communication systems these dc levels must be converted to a form which can be transmitted over a communication channel. This conversion step is typically performed by a MODEM and is termed *modulation*. The modulation most generally used is one of three types, that is, amplitude modulation (AM), frequency modulation (FM), or phase modulation (PM), although there are other types.

Amplitude modulation involves transmitting at one amplitude for a "1" and at a second amplitude for a "0". For data bit rates up to 300 bits/second, this form of modulation is adequate. For bit rates up to 2000 bits/second, FM is popular. Here two different frequency bands, centered about the modulation carrier frequency, transmit "1s" and "0s".

When bit rates exceed 4000 bits/second, phase modulation has advantages. Here the carrier is continuously transmitted, but the phase for a "1" is 0 degrees and for a "0" switch 180 degrees. Although we have referred to bits per second, the communication term here is *bauds*.

The primary determining factors as to which type of modulation to use are noise susceptibility versus cost. AM is lowest in cost but most noise susceptible. It is, therefore, lowest in baud rates. At the other extreme, PM is the most expensive but most noise tolerant. FM, of course, falls somewhere in between. Modulation forms have been combined to get more data on a channel. For example, MODEMS transmitting at 9600 baud may use both AM and FM (or PM) together over an equalized telephone line. For these or higher speeds, all aspects of the hardware must be in perfect working order. As indicated earlier, T-1 code or Manchester code are now used primarily.

7-10 MODEMS

MODEM is an acronym for the words *modulation-demodulator* and is a device that permits the transmission of digital data over communication links. Its basic function is illustrated by Fig. 7-7. A MODEM is required at both ends of the link. At the transmitter end, it accepts digital data in a bit serial form and generates one tone (subcarriers) for a "1" and another tone for a "0". These two analog tones are then applied to the modulation stage of the transmitter equipment for transmission over the link. At the receiving end, the demodulation of the tones is performed and the "1s" and "0s" of the bit stream recovered and fed to the digital processing equipment. Usually, a MODEM is a two-way device, permitting both receiving and transmitting operations.

The simple MODEM (or *data set*, as it is often called), when used on a voice line for data transmission, is often connected to a distant terminal by first dialing a telephone call. Once the connection is achieved, the data can be transmitted back and forth from the connected digital equipment involved. The connection remains in effect until broken by a normal disconnect. For the type of inquiry-response

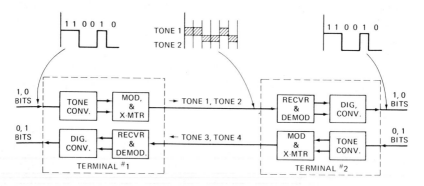

FIGURE 7-7 Basic function of a MODEM.

service required of a time-shared terminal, or where the data can be transmitted as blocks of words, this type of operation is satisfactory. However, if the system involves periodic polling of a distant terminal in an automatic mode or if it is an alarm system where distant terminals inject emergency messages to a central point, some method of automatic addressing of the terminals to be connected is necessary. Conceivably, one would not have time to personally place a connecting telephone or Teletype call.

Systems that are completely automatic in performance can be designed, but at present they are constrained by existing telephone practice. If the normal switched telephone system is employed, connections are generally made in the normal switching mode applicable to telephone voice service. In other words, achieving the connection requires from 10 sec to 3 min, depending on such factors as the telephone terminal's equipment, number of telephone exchanges, traffic, and central switches involved. Many military systems involving radio links are not quite so restricted as implied here for the telephone system. A military system can be organized as a net, so that all transceivers involved are either listening or periodically transmitting to the entire net continuously.

In the case of a station listening, it will hear a code periodically transmitted that identifies the "start" of a message. This code will alert all receivers that a message is coming and provides the synchronization of local clocks. A frame will be broadcast to the link as a bit serial message—each one word long. A possible start code is a frame of all "1s". One operating system provides five frames of all "1s", followed by one frame of all "0s".

After the start code, there are transmitted two frames of local address. These frames identify the receiver to which the message following is to be addressed and alert that particular receiver that a message is coming to its attention. The other net receivers will not accept this message but will continue to listen for their address for later messages. The message frames (as many as necessary to convey the total message) follow. These frames are then followed by two "stop" frames, which inform that the message transmission has been completed. At this point (or, on some systems, after the address phase), a verification of satisfactory transmission is returned to the original transmitting station. This return message is similar to the original transmission, but in the reverse direction, and usually consists of a one frame replay. Figure 7-8 shows possible formats for these messages.

For such a system to operate, usually one station in the net is designated to be the net-control station. In some systems all transmission back and forth between stations of the net are by permission and

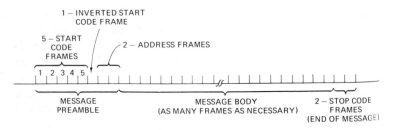

FIGURE 7-8 Message formats.

control of the net-control station. This procedure prevents chaos, such as could result if all stations were to transmit simultaneously. The net-control station will usually poll each of the other stations of the net sequentially to ascertain if any of these remote stations have, in fact, a message for net-control. This procedure has the advantage that the operating condition of all net stations remains known. If there is no message for net-control from a remote station, a negative coded replay is returned to net-control. In military systems a situation requiring an emergency message may arise; the remote station involved will be permitted to pre-empt the order by polling process, which requires then the addressing of the net-control station by the remote station, even though the call is not in its proper sequence. In the most flexible systems the designation of net-control can be assigned to any of the stations comprising the net.

Such systems as described above have been available for commercial installations since about 1973 and are still growing. If dedicated telephone lines are employed, such an automatic addressing scheme is entirely feasible today; in fact, the ASC II code is designed with this in mind.

The MODEM required for an automatic system such as outlined above is more complex than for the simple telephone data sets and must include logic for generating and decoding the control frames required for automatic addressing. In addition to this logic there is also a need for a higher level of message error detection and correction than in simpler systems. It is desirable wherever possible to reduce the necessity for repeating messages. As a consequence, error-correction codes are used to correct errors in received messages. Polynominal codes such as the Hamming code are used extensively, although other codes may be specified to react to special conditions. Where the error-correction code does not restore the message frame to an errorless message (as detected by the error-detection and correction logic), it can be designed to request a second transmission of the error-prone frame. If the error rate becomes too high, possibly because of a fading radio transmission, perhaps then the channel should be shut down and another mode of transmission adopted. Again, the MODEM should be able to detect when conditions are so bad that a reassembly accurate data message cannot get through.

MODEMS, therefore, do more than merely change the form of data. They are involved in the determination as to whether the data message is free of error and may generate and interpret control message words required for automatic addressing. In regard to the error correction and detection function, Hamming (or other) codes are generated when the MODEM transmits and, in turn, interprets these codes while receiving. The MODEM must also generate proper clocking for its internal use. This process usually involves synchronizing the local MODEM to the clock of the link—a function provided by the start code frames previously discussed. If the message bits employ a self-clocking waveform such as Manchester code, the clock can be derived from the message bit waveform. A functional view of a complex MODEM is shown in Fig. 7-9.

When a MODEM becomes as complex as indicated in Fig. 7-9 the all-inclusive term *terminal* is often substituted for MODEM. The terminal may provide the MODEM function for several types of digital equipment. This is especially true when many low-speed digital devices are to share a common communication line or link. The terminal will then include a multiplexer and demultiplexer, if required, to meet the demands of the system, as well as interfacing circuitry to each unit

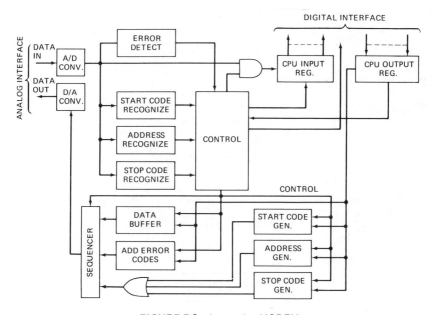

FIGURE 7-9 A complex MODEM.

of digital equipment attached to the system. This more complex apparatus is now sometimes called a *concentrater*. The foregoing is a general statement, and the exact definition and implementation varies widely in practice.

7-11 AUTOMATIC MESSAGE TRANSMISSION

For commercial systems the need for automatic digital message transmission has also been recognized. The present ASC II code standards (see Table 3-1) contain control characters which are designed to make this mode of operation practical. The message to be transmitted is organized as shown in Fig. 7-10, where the heading contains the address of the receiving station and other instructional information such as sending station identification, time of day, message number, data, etc. The SOH is a control character which signifies "start of heading". Previous to the SOH character, one or more SYN (synchronizing) control characters is sent, depending on whether synchronizing of the individual net stations is required. Following the heading is the STX control character, which signifies "start of text". The text message is then sent in either alphanumeric or binary code. The GS code immediately precedes binary data, and the FS code immediately precedes

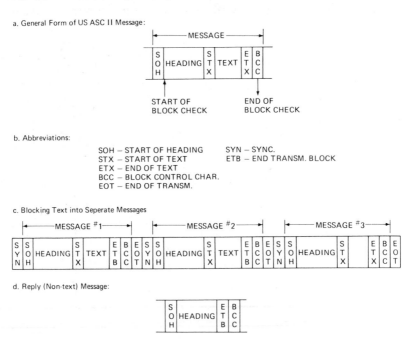

a. General Form of US ASC II Message:

b. Abbreviations:

SOH — START OF HEADING   SYN — SYNC.
STX — START OF TEXT   ETB — END TRANSM. BLOCK
ETX — END OF TEXT
BCC — BLOCK CONTROL CHAR.
EOT — END OF TRANSM.

c. Blocking Text into Seperate Messages

d. Reply (Non-text) Message:

FIGURE 7-10 ASC II formats.

alphanumeric data. Both types of data can be included in the same message. The "end of text" is indicated by the ETB control character, which is then followed by the BCC, or block check character. This character provides a vertical parity check bit on each bit column. If the present message is the last of the transmission, then the final control character is an EOT, which means "end of transmission".

Although the message format thus far provides a great deal of control for intercomputer messages, there are other capabilities to be desired. For instance, one might desire that a message be a complete recording of a link message, including control characteristics. In the system described thus far, control characters within the message are forbidden, since the terminal will recognize them as control characters and will attempt to respond. A method called *transparent transmission* allows one to send such messages by use of the control character called *data link escape* (DLE), which means that the terminal should disregard control characters following a DLE-STX character set. Thus, a message containing control character can be transmitted. To recover from the transparent transmission mode the DLE-EOT character set would be transmitted, which restores normal recognition of control characters.

Error checking in the ASC II mode employs the combination of vertical and horizontal parity, with vertical parity provided by the BCC character. In the transparent transmission mode or other special modes, Hamming code may be employed for error control purposes. In addition, if the control characters appear in an incorrect or disordered sequence, such a condition can also be detected, resulting in an error condition. The usual way to handle errors is for the receiver to request a retransmission, which is accomplished by the transmitter station's listening for a response from the receiver station after the transmitter finishes its message with an ETB or EOT character. The receiver will transmit back to the transmitter station and acknowledge ACKO or ACK1 if it passes all error checks, or NAK if it fails an error check. The appearance of NAK causes the transmitter to retransmit the original message several times until a prescribed number of NAKs are received, indicating a true failure, or until an ACK is received, indicating that the transmission was received accurately.

7-12 ERROR DETECTION AND CORRECTION

Error detection and correction is important when it is necessary to keep errors from occurring in digital data, especially during transmission between two points. Errors result when a bit is misinterpreted at the receiving end from what it actually was when transmitted. The introduction of noise, shifting time relationships between data and clock, components acting intermittently, etc., can cause such discrepancies. To obtain a degree of protection, it is common practice to add redundant bits to a message, which, in effect, provide a check at the receiver. There are many possible codes that one can apply; however, a full examination is beyond the scope of this text, so only three examples are presented here. Providing error checking and/or correcting capabilities requires additional hardware expense plus additional bits to a message—plus added time, in some instances, for implementing a check operation.

A complete study of code generation is part of the vast and highly theoretical field of communication theory. There are many ways to generate codes which are both efficient conveyors of messages and also provide efficient error detection and correction capabilities, thus permitting reliable transmission under adverse conditions. A few elementary examples follow.

7-12.1 Parity Codes

The simplest application of redundancy for detecting error is use of a parity bit. Examples of both even and odd parity are shown in Fig. 7-11. In the case of even parity a redundant bit is added (or not added) to make the count of "1s" in a word equal to an even number (0, 2, 4, 6, etc.). An odd parity bit, on the other hand, is added to a word (or not added) to make the count of "1s" an odd value (1, 3, 5, 7, etc.)

A parity bit is added at the transmitting end to provide the prescribed parity. At the receiving end the word parity is rechecked, and then it is determined if the parity criteria have been met. If the criteria have not been met, and if only one error occurs, an error is detected by the fact that the parity test fails.

Implementation of this check system is not difficult and in a completely serial system involves adding a single flip-flop at both the trans-

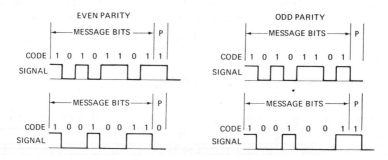

FIGURE 7-11 Establishing the parity bit (even/odd).

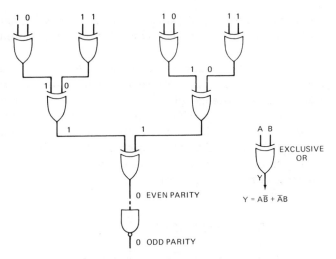

FIGURE 7-12 Parity check or generation logic.

mitting and receiving ends of the path. The transmitting end flip-flop completes an initial resetting toggle on "1s". Its final position is transmitted as an extra bit positioned at the end of the data bits. At the receiving end a second flip-flop is reset and toggled in the same way by "1s". Its final position indicates the parity and can be connected to an alarm if the parity test fails. By the use of exclusive-OR gates parity can be generated and also tested in a parallel transfer system, although more hardware is necessary. Such an example is shown by Fig. 7-12.

Now, if data is transmitted in block form (for instance, a group of characters to be stored on magnetic tape) parity can be added and

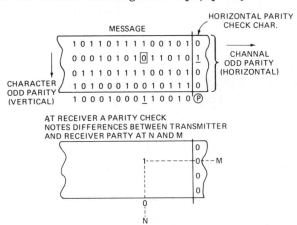

FIGURE 7-13 Block error checking.

checked both across (horizontal), on a per character basis, and downward (vertical), on a columnar basis. This method is illustrated by Fig. 7-13.

In this system a single error will cause a failure both in horizontal and vertical parity. In fact, the intersection where the failure occurs is obvious, and this knowledge points to the possibility of an error-correction method as well as an error-detection method. Knowing a particular bit is in error implies that the bit must be complemented to remove the error. More elaborate error-correcting methods are based on this general principle. In the next section we discuss one of the better known error-correction methods.

7-13 ERROR-CORRECTING CODES

Perhaps the best known of the error-correcting codes is the one attributed to Hamming, known simply as the *Hamming code*. This code employs multiple parity in which the even parity of selected groups of bits determine if an error is present and exactly which bit is in error. Thus, the ability to correct a single error is possible—even if it occurs in the check bits themselves. In the general case the addition of check bits to a word is necessary if the advantages of error correction are desired. For instance, a word having any combination of 4 bits, $X_1 X_2 X_3 X_4$, will require an addition of 3 check bits to provide an error-correction capability. The transmitted word will now be:

$$\underbrace{X_1 \ X_2 \ X_3 \ X_4}_{\text{Data}} \ \underbrace{X_5 \ X_6 \ X_7}_{\substack{\text{Error} \\ \text{correction} \\ \text{code}}}$$

The total number of correction bits for any word length can be determined from evaluating the inequality:

$$2^k \geqslant m + 1$$

where m = total data bits, k = check bits, n = total of data and check bits ($n = m + k$).

As an example of the case discussed above,

$$2^k \geqslant m + 1$$

Since $m + 1 = 5$ and if $k = 3$, $2^k = 8$. Therefore, a 3-bit error correction code is required for 4 data bits.

Now the next step is to construct k even parity equations which must have certain properties:

1. $X_a + X_b + X_c + \ldots + X_p = 0$
   (a) X_a, X_b, and X_c ... are the data bit integers and are given the value 1 or 0, depending on what the bit value is in the data bit portion of the word.
   (b) X_p is the value of the check bit ("1" or "0") and is assigned a value (1 or 0) to make the parity even for equation 1, etc.
2. The X_a, X_b, and X_c, etc, are assigned X_5, X_6, X_7, etc., in such a manner that the k equations:
   (a) Will all be different in the assignment of X_1, X_2, X_3, etc.
   (b) Each column containing X_1 or X_2 or X_3, etc., will consist of a different code of bit combinations.
   (c) The code of correction bits (X_5, X_6, X_7 in the example) will be different for each error in a particular data bit (X_1, X_2, X_3, and X_4 of the example).

For the case above, three equations that meet the criteria established are:

1. $X_1 + X_2 + X_3 + X_5 = 0$
2. $X_1 + X_2 + X_4 + X_5 = 0$
3. $X_1 + X_3 + X_4 + X_7 = 0$

Note if there are no errors, check bits X_5, X_6, or X_7 will have a value $X_5 = 0$, $X_6 = 0$, $X_7 = 0$, or 000. For any error that occurs in the transmission, a parity error will occur in one of the above equations (a "1" is generated; in fact, the code of "1s" shows what bit (1-7) is in error. For example, a code appears in Table 7-2. A code received at the receiver will have a "1" in positions X_5, X_6, or X_7. As shown, this code reports the exact bit in error and thus can be corrected by com-

TABLE 7-2

ERROR BIT CODES

Bits in Error	Error Code
None	*000*
X_1	*111*
X_2	*110*
X_3	*101*
X_4	*011*
X_5	*100*
X_6	*010*
X_7	*001*

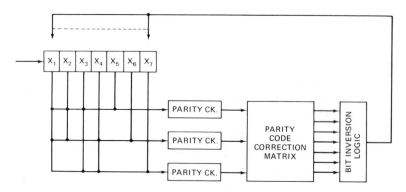

FIGURE 7-14 Hamming code detection-correction logic.

plementing it. This system is good only for one error; therefore, by using multiple parity, errors can be both detected and corrected. This is called the *Hamming detection and correction method.* Figure 7-14 illustrates this method and indicates the necessary hardware.

7-14 ERROR DETECTION AND CORRECTION: THE POLYNOMIAL APPROACH

Another, more sophisticated approach, although related to the Hamming method, differs in that error-correction bits are generated by using polynomials as follows:

$$X^{n-k} G(X) + R(X) = F(X)$$

where n = total message bits (message plus check bits), k = total message bits, and $n - k$ = total check bits. $G(X)$ is a polynomial formed of message bits, where there is a "1" in the message; that is,

$$110011 = 1xX^5 + 1xX^4 + 0xX^3 + 0xX^2 + 1xX^1 + 1xX^0$$
$$= X^5 + X^4 + X + 1$$

where $R(X)$ = the remainder when $G(X)$ is divided by a second polynominal called $P(X)$, which is the *generator polynomial.* This polynomial$^{n(x)}$ must divide evenly into the polynomial $X^{n-1} G(X) + R(X)$ whenever there are no errors transmitted to the receiving end. $F(X)$ is the polynomial transmitted to the receiver, $G(X)$ being the message bits, and $N(X)$ the error check bits. X^{n-k} merely shifts the message bits to the higher polynomial position. For the message, the highest-order bits are transmitted first.

The application of this method is best demonstrated by an elementary example. For instance, suppose that we wish to transmit a 4-bit message and use 3 check bits, such as:

$$\overbrace{\underbrace{MMMM}_{k} \overbrace{XXX}^{n-k}}^{n}$$

The $X^{n-k} = X^3$; thus, the first three columns of the table below can be formed by applying the method and using the $G(X)$ divided by $P(X)$. The fourth column is calculated by dividing the $X^{n-k} G(X)$ terms individually by $N(X)$, which we will assume to be $X^3 + X^2 + 1$. This division in each case gives column 4. Column 5 is derived directly as shown:

$$\overbrace{\underbrace{MMMM}_{k} \overbrace{XXX}^{n-k}}^{n}$$

where n = total message (plus check bits), k = message, $n - k$ = error correction bits.

Message	Polynomial	X^{n-k}	$X^{n-k} G(X)$	$X^{n-k} G(X)/P(X) = R(X)$
0000	0	X^3	0	0
0001	1		X^3	$X^2 + 1$
0010	X		X^4	$X^2 + X + 1$
0011	X + 1		$X^4 + X^3$	X
0100	X^2		X^5	X + 1
0101	$X^2 + 1$		$X^5 + X^3$	$X^2 + X$
0110	$X^2 + X$		$X^5 + X^4$	X^2
0111	$X^2 + X + 1$		$X^5 + X^4 + X^3$	1
etc.				

Now assume a generating code of $X^3 + X^2 + 1$.
Divide $X^{n-k} G(X)$ by $X^3 + X^2 + 1$.
The code $F(X)$ will be $X^{n-k} G(X) + R(X) = F(X)$.
The division process is really one of modular-add (exclusive-OR process). An example is shown in Fig. 7-15. The advantage to

Example:
To compute the error correction code for the message—0011. The message plus the error correction code will be:

$$0\ 0\ 1\ 0\ X\ X\ X$$

The message polynomial is—

$$0.X^3 + 0.X^2 + 1.X^1 + 1.X^0 = X + 1 = G(X)$$

Now:

$$X^{n-k}G(X) = X^3(X + 1) = X^4 + X^3$$

And:

$$X^{n-k}G(X)/P(X) = X^4 + X^3/X^3 + X^2 + 1 = R(X)$$

By modular division we have:

$$
\begin{array}{r}
X \\
X^3 + X^2 + 1\ )\overline{X^4 + X^3} \\
X^4 + X^3 + X \\
\hline
X = R(X)
\end{array}
$$

Therefore, the error correction code is:

$$0\ 1\ 0$$

And the message plus the error correction bits are:

$$0\ 0\ 1\ 1\ 0\ 1\ 0 \quad \text{error correction bits}$$
$$\text{msd} \quad \underline{\qquad}$$

FIGURE 7-15 Division by the modular-add method.

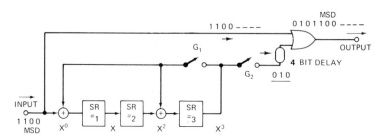

"Shift-register-modular-adder" Code Generator

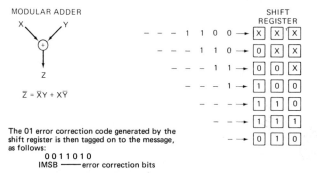

$$\overline{Z} = \overline{X}Y + X\overline{Y}$$

The 01 error correction code generated by the shift register is then tagged on to the message, as follows:

$$0\ 0\ 1\ 1\ 0\ 1\ 0$$
$$\text{IMSB} \underline{\qquad}\text{error correction bits}$$

The above shift register-modular-adder logic provides the generating polynomial $P(X) = X^3 + X^2 + 1$ and, in fact, this logic provides a hardware implementation of the modular-add division process illustrated

FIGURE 7-16 Shift register generation of error/correction codes.

this method is the case where the error-correction/detection codes can be generated and detected for a serial transmission. A shift register/modular-2 adder for the generation polynomial $R(X)$ is shown in Fig. 7-16.

In an actual system, the message bits are routed into the shift register, followed directly by $n - k$ 0's. Gate G_1 is open, and gate G_2 is shorted. Therefore, the message bits, as they leave the register to the right, are modular-2 added back into the register, as shown in the figure. The process, in effect, divides $X^{n-k} G(X)$ by $P(X)$; therefore, what is left in the register is, in reality, $R(X)$.

$R(X)$ is added to the delayed $G(X)$ to obtain $F(X)$, which is transmitted. Figure 7-16 illustrates the general process.

At the receiving end, the $X^{n-k} G(X)$ portion can be used to calculate $R(X)$ by similar logic. The $R(X)_T$ transmitter and the $R(X)_c$ determined can be compared, and if a difference is noted that is a clue indicating that an error has occurred. The difference between $R(X)_T$ and $R(X)_c$ can be compared in a table which identifies which bit is in error, thus permitting error correction to be applied. The receiving-end equipment is similar to that of the transmitting end but does require the additional comparison and table lookup process indicated.

7-15   THE ARPA LINK FOR COMPUTER INTERCONNECTION

In 1972, the U.S. Advanced Research Project Agency (ARPA) inaugurated a cross-country data network to connect several university laboratory computers as far apart as Boston and Los Angeles. At each computer site there is a separate data link processor, called an *information transmission processor* (IMP), which allows all computers at the various universities to communicate with one another over the links, using a standardized format at 50 kilobits/second. Much of this technology was developed by the Defense Communications Agency Worldwide Communication AUTODIN network, which was a pioneer system. Honeywell DDP516 computers were the IMPs selected. Figure 7-17 is a diagram of this early network updated to 1978.

7-16   COMMERCIAL LINKS TODAY (1980)

As mentioned in Section 7-5, AT&T experimented during the 1960s with a digitized voice system called T-1. This system could be used for long distance transmission, even though the original T-1 network was designed only for an 0.6 mile transmission. This is, of course, history

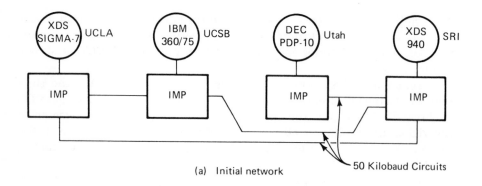

(a)   Initial network

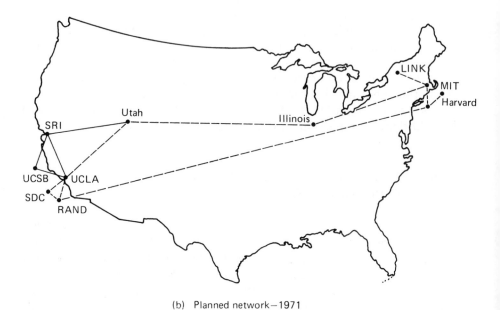

(b)   Planned network—1971

FIGURE 7-17   ARPA network in 1980.

now, but AT&T had, even before, the ARPA system, transmitted at a 50,000 bits/second with the newer line MODEMs.

Many messages can be multiplexed; thus, 50,000 bits/second intercity transmissions are now common, as typified by the ARPA network mentioned previously. At this time, one can only speculate as to the nature of future techniques such as fiber optics and other faster transmission methods now in the planning stages.

Table 7-3 lists many of the desirable features of optimum transmission systems. Several features have already been mentioned; others are discussed in this section and the next two chapters.

TABLE 7-3

TYPICAL USES OF DATA COMMUNICATIONS

Common Teleprocessing Usage Modes	Specific Application Examples	Distinguishing Characteristics of Typical Transactions
Source data entry data collection	*Sales-status data; inventory control; payroll data gathering*	*Transactions collected several times per day or week, direct response message not issued for every transaction.*
	Point-of-sale system; airline reservations	*Transactions arrive frequently (every few seconds) and demand response within a few seconds.*
Remote batch processing, remote job entry	*Remote-city high-speed card reading and printing; inexpensive local access to expensive distant computer power*	*Transactions usually are bunched and require processing times ranging from minutes to hours; input and output for each transaction individually may take seconds or minutes.*
Information retrieval	*Credit checking; bank account status; insurance policy status; law enforcement; state government social services; hospital information systems*	*Relatively low character volume per input transaction, response required within seconds; output message lengths usually very short for status inquiries, vary widely for other types of applications.*
Conversational time-sharing	*General problem solving; engineering design calculations; text editing*	*Conversational response required, usually within a few seconds.*
Message switching	*Intracompany electronic mail; delivery and memo distribution*	*Delivery time requirements range from minutes to hours.*
Real-time data acquisition and process control	*Numerical control of machine tools; remote meter and gauge reading*	*Remote sensors are continuously sampled and monitored at widely varying time intervals.*
Interprocessor data exchange	*Processor, program, and file-sharing applications of all types involving communications between computers; interorganizational networks*	*Infrequent, bursty arrivals consisting of large data blocks requiring transmission to another CPU, usually within milliseconds.*

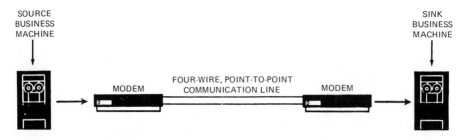

SOURCE
BUSINESS
MACHINE

SINK
BUSINESS
MACHINE

MODEM

FOUR-WIRE, POINT-TO-POINT
COMMUNICATION LINE

MODEM

FIGURE 7-18 Illustration of a relatively simple network.

One common variation of a communication network is shown in Fig. 7-18, namely, a point-to-point network connection directly between two signal conditioner terminals, SC1 and SC2.

A much more complex network is illustrated in Fig. 7-19, where more than one form of network is shown. The network connecting the input terminal of the system to information channel 1 is again a simple point-to-point segment. However, information channel 1 has two DPTE terminals (drop-point terminal equipment), each connecting separately to several sets of terminals. Channel 1 continues on to signal conditioners (SC1 and SC2) of information channel 1. Also in the system is a multipoint segment which, for purposes of illustration, has two paths. To provide redundancy in case of a path failure, the DPTE of path 1 and path 2 are interconnected; this is their only function. DPTE 3 has several terminals connected to it, as well as channel 2 and SC3 and SC4. Information path 2 connects to DPTE 1, as indicated in Fig. 7-19, and supplies information channel 3. DPTE 4 is supplied by information path 2 and has several channels as outputs. Also, channel 3 is interconnected, as well as SC3 and SC5.

Before 1969 AT&T prohibited user hardware connections to their lines except through Bell Telephone MODEM. In January 1969 AT&T revised its tariffs and permitted customer devices to be connected to their lines, with the following qualifications (prior to that time the only exceptions were certain U.S. military and other government services and transportation systems):

1. The customer's equipment was restricted in output power and energy levels, so as not to interfere or harm the network in any way.
2. The interconnection to the public switched network must be made via a telephone company device to ensure protection of the network.

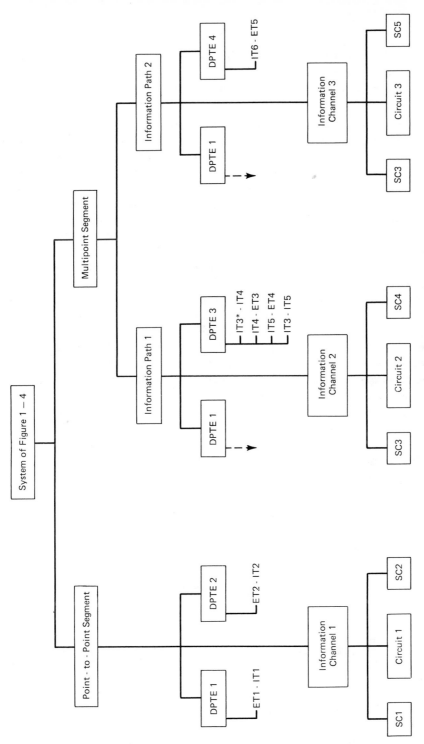

FIGURE 7-19 A more complex system than that of Fig. 7-18.

173

3. All network control signaling must be provided with telephone company equipment, including busy signals, dialing, ringing, etc., at the connection point.

There were numerous objections to these conditions, but Bell responded by applying similar protective provisions to their leased lines as well. In 1976 the Federal Communications Commission (FCC) decided to review the entire situation and determined, in effect, that AT&T restrictions were unfair and too severe; a final decision is yet to be made. This problem has arisen because of the complexity of terminals and the need to know how total control of network switching is best achieved. The examples that follow further interpret and expand on this problem.

Figure 7-20 illustrates a dialed backup system for added reliability of an extra possible path.

Another variation is a polled network, where one computer queries the terminals to determine what traffic is necessary. City A controls the network by asking each MODEM terminal in turn at cities B, C, and D if there is indeed traffic. Normally, cities that are close together, geographically speaking, have a higher priority for communication between themselves than those more widely separated. Figure 7-21 illustrates a polled network.

Another possible variation is a multiport network with all MODEMs interconnected and communicating directly with each other and having several attached terminals. Thus, the variations are almost endless. These experimental networks continue to develop separately from

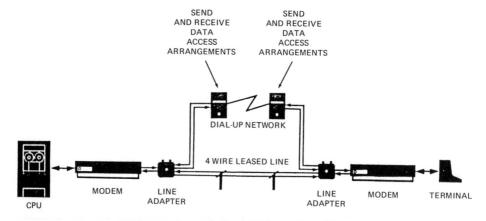

FIGURE 7-20 A leased system with dialed backup.

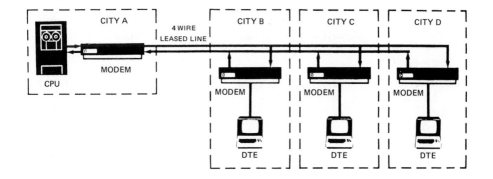

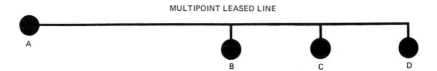

FIGURE 7-21 A polled network.

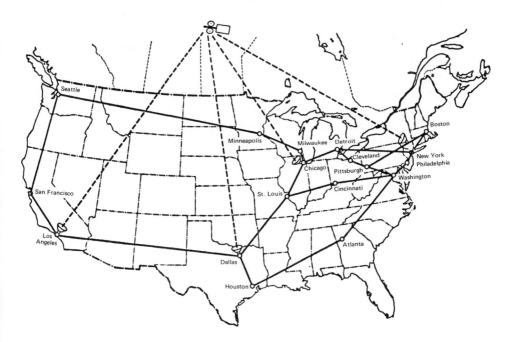

FIGURE 7-22 An early intracontinental data network.

TABLE 7-4

COMPARISON OF RS232C, RS422, AND RS423

Characteristics	RS232C	RS422	RS423
Max. line length	100 ft	5000 ft	5000 ft
Max. bit rate	2×10^4	1×10^6	1×10^5
Drivers	1.5–36 V	TTL levels	TTL levels
Min. received input	1.5 V, single ended	100 mV (diff.)	100 mV (diff.)

AT&T, which is still restricted by its original responsibility of providing voice transmission. An early data transmission network is shown in Fig. 7-22.

7-17 SUMMARY

This chapter summarizes the important aspects of communication links as they influence data communication. Since, in most cases, data travels a portion of the way over what was originally voice-grade facilities, the limitations imposed by voice grade can be controlling and must be taken into account by the use of the proper techniques and equipment. In many ways communication links and computers are not compatible, but impressive strides are being made to minimize the problems. In fact, in 1979 many networks were established for data transmission alone. Important techniques of multiplexing, both FDM and TDM, are superimposing more message capacity on common networks. In fact, some transmission is already taking place via satellites, and fiber optics networks are in advanced planning stages or in initial usage.

There are new standards for serial transmission that allow higher bit rates and longer distance transmission. These standards are compared with RS232C in Table 7-4.

8

Special Systems

8-1 INTRODUCTION

This chapter covers a variety of details to complete the discussion of interfacing and also includes several digital systems not yet covered. Section 8-2 is an introduction to distributed systems, now becoming increasingly popular. Section 8-3 covers the various aspects of time-sharing operations in some detail. Section 8-4 concerns the time-sharing language BASIC, which is easy to use for writing programs and in some versions, such as that furnished by Hewlett-Packard, is as versatile as the generally considered compilers COBOL and FORTRAN. Section 8-5 describes a minicomputer system used to control power plants. It has two minicomputers, each performing separate tasks but in the end assisting one another. The chapter concludes with examples of some of the standard microcomputer buses: these are preliminary; improved versions or completely new ones will be proposed in the future.

8-2 DISTRIBUTED SYSTEMS

Distributed systems involve multiconnected processors which may require combinations of large machines (called *mainframes*) or combinations of minicomputers by themselves or combinations of minicomputers and microcomputers. Individual processors communicate (transfer data and instructions) with one another. When these processors are in close proximity they are termed *multicomputers,* but when they are located hundreds of feet or miles apart they are termed *interconnected multiple processors.* These processors are linked by miles of communications network (such as SAGE and AUTODIN, the military communications data network, which require data communication back and forth from distant processors or terminals via communication links).

A very practical application of interconnected multiple processors appeared during recent studies of communication technical control techniques. In a typical system a central computer is required at a major communication switching station to provide operation of station displays (including several CRT displays), provide access to a station data base (disk file), and access the status of communication lines, trunks, and equipment associated with the station. Because of the diffused organization of a communication switching station, it is likely that much of its equipment will be located remotely from the central processor. As a consequence, line and equipment monitoring at a remote point appears to be most effectively accomplished by a satellite processor, which sequences the line and equipment testing at the remote point. If there are equipment or system failures, this information is reported by the satellite computer to the central computer. The central computer may then command the satellite processor to operate in a different mode until the failure is eliminated or other corrective action taken.

Such a system as the above has the advantage that the central processor is not required to sequence operations over the entire breadth of the system. In a sense, it delegates responsibility. This delegation process eases the overall task of generating programs for the central computer and permits system modifications with a lesser amount of specialized reprogramming. The possibility of building a system on a modular hardware and software basis is much enhanced.

The problems of interconnected multiple processors involves those of reliable data communication, addressing, and synchronizing the widely dispersed equipment. Because telephone lines are typically limited as to bandwidth, data transfer rates are typically in the 2400 bit/second region; however, newer modulation techniques employed with the MODEMs are doubling and quadrupling this rate. Presently, the need for a standardized addressing method to automatically interconnect and disconnect the appropriate processors is required. This interconnection/disconnection process must be universally applicable and enable proper synchronization of the end devices. An important step in this direction has been the widespread adoption of ASC II code

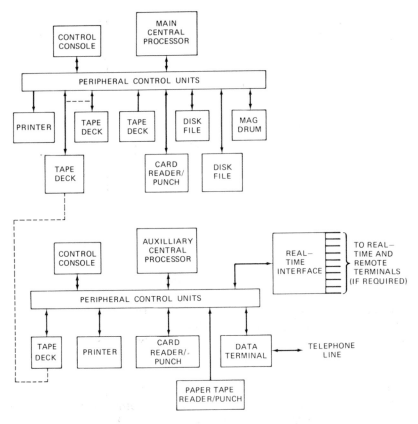

FIGURE 8-1 A distributed computer system.

with both its alphanumeric and control characters. Still, standardized headers including addressing, data error detection and correction, and message start and stop designators must be universally adopted. It appears that, to date, the military has progressed further in regard to standardization than have commercial organizations. A distributed computer system is illustrated by Fig. 8-1.

8-3 TIME-SHARED SYSTEMS

8-3.1 Introduction

A time-sharing processor system is one where several users share the use of the same processor at the same time, but each user has individual access to the processor. Often, the users are located at remote terminals some distance from the centrally located processor. Access

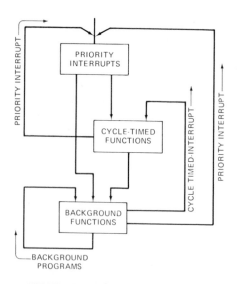

FIGURE 8-2 Basic time-shared system.

to the processor, its memory, and its files is via a communication link such as a telephone line between the central processor and the user. The basic configuration items are illustrated by Fig. 8-2.

Time-sharing systems can be divided into categories, namely, (1) monitoring systems, (2) inquiry systems, (3) multiuser systems, and (4) interactive systems. The first type of system is represented by a processor-controlled trunk line and station equipment monitors such as SATEC (semiautomatic technical control). With SATEC the test system sensing a failure of a communication path (trunk line) to a distant point to adhere to specified operating tolerances causes an alarm reaction. Such phenomena as excessive circuit noise or low signal strength may activate the alarm. A central operator sitting at a CRT console will call up additional data about the sensitive condition and then can access the stored files for instructions as to what procedures to follow. Usually, more than one operator has access to the files in a SATEC application; hence, there will be more than one person using the processor in a time-sharing mode. Figure 8-3 illustrates briefly the SATEC system concept, although in recent years it has been superseded by a newer concept, that of completely automated control, called ATEC.

Another function of a time-sharing system is represented by American Airlines' SABRE reservation system, one of the first commercial time-sharing systems installed anywhere. This system allows widely dispersed ticket agents to inquire of a central reservation file as to the status of prescribed flight throughout the American Airlines system. A local reservation clerk can enter updated information, based upon what services a customer requires, such as requesting advance space, fare in-

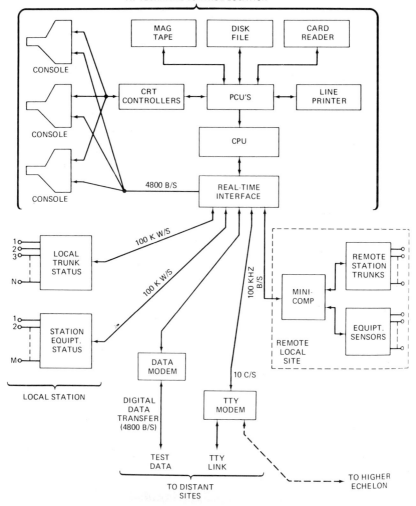

FIGURE 8-3 The SATEC system.

formation, interconnecting flights to specific destinations, etc. The system supplies the requested information immediately. A brief illustration of this system appears in Fig. 8-4.

The third type of time-sharing system is the one most commonly associated with time-sharing and is illustrated by Fig. 8-5. In this system individual users insert programs from their terminals into the central processor. These programs are stored, perhaps in a disk file, until the user calls for them, whether that be immediately or after a period of time. When the user decides to use the stored program, the user supplies the needed data from his or her terminal. The results of the

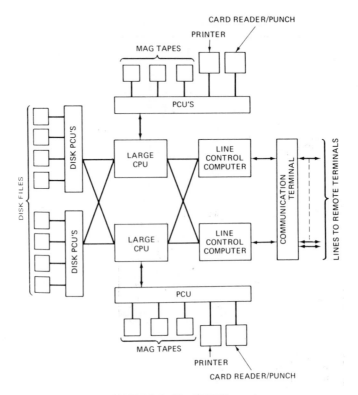

FIGURE 8-4 The SABRE system.

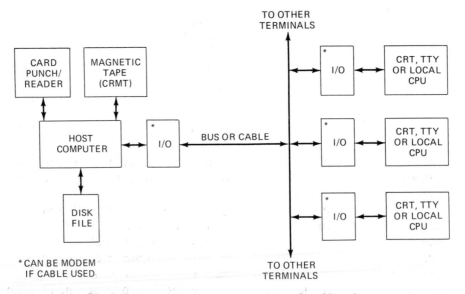

FIGURE 8-5 An interactive local system, as found in a plant.

program execution are returned to the user at the remote terminal, usually in a few seconds.

A fourth type, often a local plant-dedicated system, is an interactive system, where several operators at different consoles share the same design program. This system is similar to type (3), but without the necessity of leased telephone line connections. Systems of this kind are used for graphic design rather than for the purpose of running arbitrary programs. For example, the display consoles generate line drawings and general drafting.

8-3.2 Time-Sharing Services

Time-sharing service began in 1965 on a commercial basis. In 1963 the first successful system was developed at the Massachusetts Institute of Technology (MIT's Project MAC), and a second one was to follow shortly thereafter at Dartmouth College. The time-sharing compiler BASIC, written for the Dartmouth system, has since been improved and is one of the most popular time-sharing compiler languages available because it is relatively easy to learn. BASIC is now very popular in programming all types of minicomputers and microcomputers, being continually upgraded for new applications. Hewlett-Packard has updated BASIC applying it to business applications once the province of COBOL only.

Despite its modest beginnings, time-sharing has been one of the fastest growing of all processor applications. By the end of 1968 there were about 53 installations throughout the country, with many of the giants of the industry (General Electric Company, International Business Machines, Scientific Data Systems, Computer Sciences Corporation, and Honeywell Inc., etc.) participating. Also, a flood of new organizations appeared including Tyme-share, Inc., University Computing, Dial Data, and numerous others. Many corporations installed private nationwide systems. A typical local plant system is shown in Fig. 8-5.

It is difficult to predict at this time the potential scope of applications adaptable to time-sharing systems. Thus far there has been extensive usage for reservation systems in the transportation and hotel industries. Scientific use has also broadened, with scientists and engineers using time-sharing to solve problems adaptable to program-oriented languages such as BASIC and conversational FORTRAN. For example, a problem, equations, and data are written in conventional FORTRAN form, forwarded via a communication link to the processor, and a solution in printout form is returned to the user in due time by a return path. This service has a decided advantage over batch processing in that the user can submit corrections or modifications from his or her console without the necessity of taking a new IBM card or two over to the processor, probably some distance away. Other types of problems of a design nature are graphical in form. Here the operator can accomplish a form of drafting on the CRT scope face (or other graphical forms for which a CRT is best known) and then can erase or add lines as necessary. By drawing more than one plan view, an operator can by the program request a display of the design rotated about any axis; thus, a form of three-dimensional picture is obtained. The operator here is truly interacting with the computer program.

Information retrieval processes can be implemented with time-sharing systems. Here the user would request via command a document which would then be displayed to the user page by page via a CRT. This possibility alone has a tremendous value to business, education, science, law, and many other phases of human activity.

In the field of text editing, a page can be typed into a CRT, and then lines, words, or complete paragraphs erased, or text can readily be amended without resorting to a pen or erasure. The text page reforms itself after each editing step, and the final version of the page can be stored until needed.

In the field of education, many experiments in time-sharing have been conducted. A student can request lessons, which are displayed via a CRT. The machine submits questions to the student and awaits answers. Depending on each answer, the system will submit the next question. On the basis of the pattern of right or wrong answers, a set of questions will vary in depth and number. Thus, students may progress as rapidly or as slowly as their capabilities permit.

Other uses of time-shared systems involve testing and control of industrial processes, of communication systems, of traffic control, of business invoicing, and many other activities.

Even batch processing is not to be ignored. Here a user can submit card decks, magnetic tapes, etc., via peripherals located at remote terminals having the required capabilities, and the data is forwarded via a communication link to a centrally located processor. At the central processor the data is processed in a batching mode as it would be at a normally operated computer center, but the actual physical input of data occurs miles away at the user locations. The computed results are returned also via a link and displayed at the user's terminal or input to magnetic tape for later display. In this type of operation Teletype terminals are replaced by tape-handling equipment (either paper or magnetic), which are capable of data-handling rates limited only by the communication line bandwiths rather than by the speeds of the terminals and computer peripherals themselves.

There are many features essential to a successful time-sharing system, and the more important of these are discussed individually in the following sections.

8-3.3 Memory Protection

A user's program must be protected from encroachment (destruction or alteration of one's program) by another user who does not have authorized access to that program. Such protection is accomplished usually by one of three methods: (1) hardware registers which define the boundary limits of a user's program and will not permit access beyond the addresses specified by these registers; (2) assignment of a protective key which the program user must possess; or (3) software protection, where the limits of the program memory assignment is specified by the program and that fact is checked before each instruction is performed. In any case, the user is limited to an assigned memory space, and other users are not permitted to encroach.

8-3.4 User Independence

Each user must be enabled to use the system for independent application and not be influenced by other users. Users inherently should feel that the computer is theirs alone. To provide this feature, access must be provided with little delay, sufficient memory space must be supplied, and the correct results returned without undue delays. Since the computer's resources are not infinite (memory and processor time are limited) and many users could well be requesting service at the same time, a well thought out system design is necessary to avoid undue delays for users. Often, a time limit for operation of any one program is established. If the program is not finished within that time it is temporarily terminated and returned to the bulk-store (disk file) memory, where it is placed at the end of the line of waiting programs. The next program to be serviced is transferred in from the disk file, and it is then run the allotted time. If it is not completed it is also returned to the end of the line (queue) to await its turn again. In this manner all programs have an allotment of time in the processor. In some systems priorities can be established to alter this arbitrary sequence.

8-3.5 Supervisor Program

A supervisor (executive) program must exist to provide each user the space and time allocations discussed in the last two sections. In addition, the supervisor program will accept the service request interrupts from the user terminals. It will allocate the necessary central peripherals and provide for reallocation of the user programs in memory files in order that the most efficient use of the available internal memory will occur. The supervisor program always resides in the internal memory, while the user program will alternate between the internal memory and the bulk-store files, as determined by the time and algorithms. The supervisor program is protected in the sense that it cannot be modified either accidentally or on purpose by any user.

8-3.6 Interrupt Systems

The interrupt system provides the processor and peripherals a means of obtaining service from the supervisor program. The types of available service include:

1. Interrupts from the peripherals to indicate completion of an assigned task.
2. Interrupts from the consoles to indicate that improper services or input requested by the operator.
3. Interrupts at the end of the allotted time of program runs or the completion of programs.
4. Interrupts caused by error detection, program overflows, power failures, and other causes relating to system errors.

The supervisor program will evaluate these interrupts and decide on the next action to take. In the case of type 3, the calling-up of a diagnostic program is a strong possibility.

8-3.7 Memory Allocation

There must be a technique for orderly allocation and control of both the internal memory and bulk-store memory between user programs. One popular scheme is to split the memory into fixed-length segments called *pages*. These pages are located, transferred, and scattered throughout memory as units. Special logic is required to control the paging system, and a section of memory or a separate control memory is devoted to a table which contains the addresses of all page segments belonging to each program. If the table indicates a page is not located in core memory and is needed for the program in progress, the paging logic issues a request (interrupt) to the supervisor program, which will then look for and retrieve the missing page from the bulk-store file. During this process it may be necessary to transfer temporarily back to the bulk-store a page presently in core of calculations accomplished previously.

Fortunately, the programmer does not have to worry about these details. In addition to easing the record keeping of lengthy program location lists, further advantages are claimed such as lightening the programming task and allowing the process or program to concentrate only on arithmetic-type operations.

The lower visibility of program operation control is obtained by an increase in hardware, however. As an example, the GE 645 requires 11 specialized registers and the IBM 360/67 requires 16 special registers which are employed solely for controlling the starting and stopping of programs within allocated limits.

Another system of allocation is used for some computers, but the method entails a delay in the user's program execution. This system employs a *basic address* register, which stores originally the first address of the program to be executed. This register is incremented at each program step, thereby calling successive instructions. At the completion of the present program other programs in core are regrouped in the memory available (a process called *packing*), and the next program is started by reloading the basic address register with the initial address of the next program. The next program then proceeds from the new starting point, again in an incrementing mode.

8-3.8 Hardware Features

The appropriate processor to use for a time-sharing operation depends primarily on what the particular system is required to do. Almost all processors can be used to some extent for time-sharing; however, those especially designed for this service are usually more efficient. For example, a sufficient interrupt capability is required. Also, a buffered channel to access the bulk-store memories is usually necessary, so as not to overload the processor or slow it down by frequent transfer operations. A means of memory allocation is required, whether it be paging, base address registers, or other suitable techniques. In addition to these features, the following hardware functions are necessary.

A Large Core Memory and Fast Processor. If the core memory is too small, it will be unable to retain both the supervisor program and the user programs effectively. This condition leads to excessive paging transfers, thus reducing the time devoted to actual processing.

A Real-time Clock. This feature is necessary to allocate the program time among the users and is also required to determine a user's total operating time and thereby a user's operating costs in commercial systems.

A Versatile Bulk-store. Several types of bulk-store may be desirable. Disk files are effective for paging operations, but their access time is in milliseconds. System throughput would increase dramatically in many instances if economical bulk-store systems with a microsecond access were available. One technique that is used occasionally is to couple both disk files and magnetic drums together into a system. A drum generally has an average access time of about 20% of a disk file; hence, as many pages as possible are stored in the drum. Another technique to speed up program accessing is to use a parallel organization to connect all peripheral devices to both the processor and the communication terminal. Transfers between the bulk-sotre on the communication line can then bypass the processor completely.

Communication Line Terminals. Since most time-sharing systems involve transfer of information to or from users via communication lines, connecting communication devices such as MODEMs, multiplexers, or concentraters are required. The choice of such devices (usually called *terminals*) is usually based on their technical features and their cost. Because one of the major expenses to a user is the type of communication service employed, it behooves a system manager to carefully evaluate the minimal communication services and equipment required. Reliability of an entire time-sharing system can be a function of how well the processor-communication link and terminal-communication link interface is established and also of the capability of the communication facilities to provide an error-free data path. The use of error-correction codes or other message verifying methods can well be a system requirement with specifications defining the maximum acceptable error rate.

User Terminals. Teletype equipment has long been the workhorse of time-sharing terminals, but since the basic transmission rate of this equipment is 10 to 15 characters per second, other methods are often desired to obtain greater data transfer rates. Faster Teletype equipment

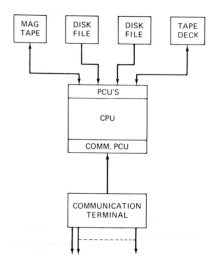

FIGURE 8-6 Series organization of peripherals.

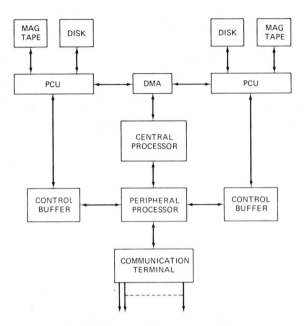

FIGURE 8-7 Parallel access to peripherals.

is available, and therefore a factor when considering system capabilities. Two accompanying figures show two possible ways to connect peripherals. Figure 8-6 features a serial transfer. In Fig. 8-7 the transfer time is greatly improved, since the processor is not positioned between the bulk-store and the communication terminal. In this particular system a separate satellite processor handles the communication line swiftly and provides other control features. This type of system is extremely powerful, since the task of controlling the user interface is delegated completely away from the central processor.

8-4 A LANGUAGE FOR TIME-SHARING

8-4.1 General

The language BASIC permits a terminal operator to interact (put in commands and read out results) at a time-sharing Teletype terminal. Because the time-shared computer completes the action for each statement and may require operator response, the language is *not* called a *compiler* but is known as an *interpreter*. Minicomputers effectively use BASIC as a compiler.

Although conversational versions of many compiler languages exist for time-sharing operations, including *conversational* FORTRAN, the occasional user of a time-sharing system does not usually need the power and sophistication of a professional-level compiler language; instead, a language that is effective but easy to learn and to use is sufficient. Such a language is BASIC, developed at Dartmouth College for use with its time-sharing system. Because of space limitations here, only a few brief comments and examples are provided. Also, as time advances, even this simple interpretive compiler is continually being upgraded as to its limited capabilities. BASIC is essentially a simplified FORTRAN. The symbols used in BASIC consist generally of multiplication, division, addition, subtraction, and exponent manipulation.

The types of statements allowed in BASIC are briefly tabulated in Table 8-1. This approach is used to present the essential material as

TABLE 8-1

EXAMPLES OF BASIC STATEMENTS

Statement Type	Form	Use
LET	LET ⟨variable⟩ = expression	Assigns values to variables.
PRINT	PRINT ⟨ expression or message ⟩,	. . . Print variable, constants, formulas, etc.
END	END	Last statement.
GO TO	GO TO ⟨statement number⟩	Transfer control to statement designated.
READ	READ ⟨variable list⟩	Reads in data; assigns first data variable to first data statement, etc.
DATA	DATA ⟨variable list⟩	Defines data values.
INPUT	INPUT ⟨variable list⟩	Inputs number from keyboard.
IF THEN	IF ⟨expression⟩ operator ⟨expression⟩ THEN ⟨statement number⟩	Tests for an inequality; transfers control on the basis of test results; operators included are: $<$, less than $>$, greater than $<=$, less or equal to $>=$, greater or equal to $=$, equal to $<>$ not equal to
FOR	FOR ⟨variable⟩ = expression to expression step	Sets the control condition for a multilisting loop.

TABLE 8-1 (cont)

Statement Type	Form	Use
NEXT	NEXT ⟨variable⟩	Returns loop to start.
DIM	DIM $n(a_1, a_2)$, $m(b_1, b_2)$	Defines dimensions of matrix n and m; a_1, a_2, b_1, b_2 are the respective dimensions of the two matrices.

Statement types defined:

STOP	—stops operations at once
RUN	—begins computation or program
SCRATCH	—destroys present program being run
LIST	—causes a listing output of the present program
LISTxxx	—causes a list printout beginning at xxx

Also, many mathematical functions are available to the programmer. These include:

SIN(x)	—sine of x	Add	= +
COS(x)	—cosine of x	Subtract	= −
TAN(x)	—tangent of x	Multiply	= *
ATN(x)	—arc tangent of x	Divide	= /
and several others of a similar nature.		Raise to power	= ↑

compactly as possible. Other miscellaneous statements included in BASIC but not tabulated include:

REM: used to insert remarks.

DEF: used to define functions in a program.

RND: used to automatically generate random numbers.

GOSUB: used to enter a subroutine.

RETURN: used to return to statement following GOSUB.

RESTORE: used to reread data more than once in a program.

For control purposes, statements are provided that are typed by the operator while using the console. These statements with their function are listed in Table 8-1.

In addition, BASIC has a built-in function to manipulate matrices. These statements include such features as sizing the matrix, adding matrices, multiplying matrices, inverting matrices, and printing matrices. The reader is referred here to the more thorough texts* on BASIC for instructions on how to write and use these techniques.

---

*Dekossi, C. J., *Learning BASIC Fast*. Reston, VA: Reston Publishing Company, Inc., 1974.

In any practical time-sharing system there are variations of these statements, and some may either be omitted or others added. The potential user must study the instructions for a particular system to know its applications and limitations.

8-4.2 Simple Examples

To use a time-shared system from a remote console, the operator dials the computer by use of a special telephone number. The computer responds by typing a reply by Teletype and requests identification. The operator types in the identification, and if it is valid the computer replies, READY. The operator now can run the program. Assuming that the program is to be written in BASIC, the operator types the word BASIC. The computer replies with a READY.

Let us assume that the problem is to find the hypotenuse of a right triangle. The operator types out the following program:

    10   LET X = 5
    20   LET Y = 1
    30   LET HI = SQR (X↑2 + Y↑2)
    40   PRINT THE HYPOTENUSE IS HI
    50   END

Step 50 completes the simple program insertion. To run the program the operator types RUN. The computer then responds with:

THE HYPOTENUSE IS 5.099
READY

The READY indicates that the computer is ready to receive a new instruction from the operator. If the operator is through, the instruction SCRATCH and OUT is typed, which both erases the program and turns the system off. If the operator is not through, the program can be given other instructions instead, such as new values for X and Y:

    10   LET X = 10
    20   LET Y = 10
    RUN

The computer replies:

THE HYPOTENUSE IS 14.142
READY

This is a truly interactive system. The operator can modify and continue at whatever speed is desirable. By a SCRATCH of the original program, it can be rewritten so that the three values of the hypotenuse are printed:

10   READ X, Y

20   PRINT THE HYPOTENUSE IS SQR(X↑2 + Y↑2)

30   GO TO 10

40   DATA 1, 1, 5, 1, 3, 4

50   END

The revision will cause a printout of:

THE HYPOTENUSE IS 1.414

THE HYPOTENUSE IS 5.099

THE HYPOTENUSE IS 5.000

This will be followed by an error message indicating that the program has run out of data.

Although this illustration is brief, it should indicate the general procedure to a beginner and the simplicity of using a program like BASIC. A more experienced programmer might prefer to use conversational FORTRAN or other available languages. Most time-sharing systems provide a choice of many languages and operational programs that are suited to special problems and clientele. Although many computers use BASIC as a compiler, that does not limit its use to time-sharing systems.

8-5   COMPUTER CONTROL OF A COMBINED-CYCLE POWER PLANT

A modern example of minicomputer control involves combined-cycle power plants that use gas turbines and steam technology but employ gas converted from coal to fire the boilers. This system has many advantages, including no dependence on oil, low capital investment cost per kilowatt of power generation, low daily operating cost, and a low level of air pollution. A standardized control system is available to start the plant, synchronize it to the line, control turbine blade positions, regulate steam throttling pressure, load the units automatically, monitor the line outputs, and provide for automatic shutdown if conditions warrant. In October, 1977, there were seven of these plants either on-line or in the planning stage in the United States or Mexico. Figure 8-8 shows a diagram of the basic control system.

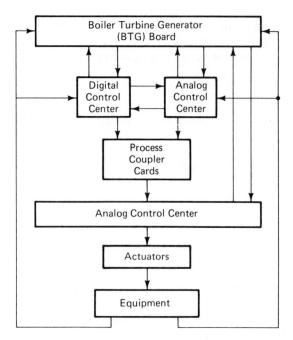

FIGURE 8-8 Combined-cycle power plant basic control system block diagram.

Analog control is necessary for actuators that control equipment. Digital control is supplied from the computers to interface with analog circuits, operate the generator board display, and accept digital converted inputs from control and monitoring. There are two minicomputers in the system's digital control center. One monitors, collects data, and performs supervisory functions, while the second is assigned to all control functions in the plant. The first unit has a disk mass memory of 500,000 words for storing various files and program software. The two computers are connected via a data link, and control information is sent to the data computer for monitoring functions, logging, and display purposes. The digital control center is shown by Fig. 8-9 and functions generally as indicated above.

For many years electric utilities have used computers to scan loads on lines and buses. Also observed automatically is the condition of equipment such as breakers, generators, and, in general, monitoring of the entire system. The effect of changing loads on various output lines, on individual generators, and other sources of power input/output of the system must be monitored for both safety and for economic reasons. A major change during the 1970s was to replace analog simulators of the 1930s with digital processors and programs that controlled, monitored, and recorded system conditions, including the performance

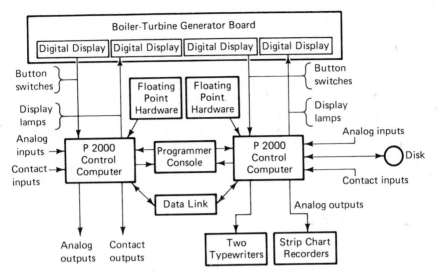

FIGURE 8-9 Digital control center block diagram.

of key transformers and the observance of transients and their effect on the system and equipment.

The explanation of these figures appears in an excellent article on pages 36–41 of the October, 1977, *IEEE Spectrum.* For complete details the reader is referred to that article: *Computer Control of Combined-cycle Power Plants* by Robert Uram of the Westinghouse Electric Corporation.

8-6 MICROCOMPUTER STANDARD BUSES

8-6.1 General

In the early days of minicomputers, there was no such thing as a standard parallel interface. Each manufacturer's version varied as to the bit lengths of the interface words, and also as to whether or not they employed an address bus. For example, Honeywell, after acquiring Control Data Corporation, adapted the 16-bit bus arrangement of the DDP116 for their models DDP416, DDP516, and H316. Although the necessity for standardization had been recognized for a long time by the military and by the telephone companies, with their Baudot and ASC II codes, little had been done. An exception was IBM's standardized 7-bit tape formats (8 including parity), later advanced to a 9-bit standard. The military had their Mil. Std. 188 (now Mil. Std. 13350). With the advent of microprocessors, standards were proposed so that the manufacturers could build interfacing boards. Some of the present models are covered briefly in the following sections.

8-6.2 S100 (Altair Bus)

This standard resulted from a conference in 1976, having been designed originally for interfacing the Intel 8080 microprocessor. This device originally had a 100-line bus, 4 voltages, a ground, 8-vectored interrupts, 8 out data lines, 8 in data lines, 2 clock lines, 4 unidentified lines, and the remainder strobes such as disable and enable. The S100 is a complete interface system, although somewhat complex, and enabled the manufacturer to build interface boards for the Intel computers.

8-6.3 MC6800 Bus

This standard accomplished the same thing for the Motorola microprocessors as the S100 bus did for the Intel 8080. It was a well-designed standard, being much simpler than the S100 bus. It has 16 individual address lines, a $\emptyset$ 2 clock, 8 bidirectional data lines, 8 strobe and control lines, and a ground.

8-6.4 IEEE Standard 488 Bus

This bus was first issued in 1974 by Hewlett-Packard for the interconnection of their instruments. It originally consisted of 25 lines. In 1975 it was much simplified to meet microprocessor requirements. The data and address information were placed on the same bidirectional bus. In addition, there were 3 lines (DAV, NRSD, and NDAC) for databyte transfer control, and 8 lines for general interface management (such as "handshaking", common mode control, etc.) This standard was updated in 1977.

8-6.5 CAMAC Dataway Bus

This is the most comprehensive bus and permits parallel data transfers up to 24 bits in parallel. It has 3 control lines, 5 address lines, 24 readout lines, 24 write lines, and 2 status lines. Not only are the bus connections standardized, but so are the voltages, the cabinets, and the racks. It is very fast, accommodating 24×10^6 bit transfers per second.

8-6.6 Future Standards

The developments in standardization continue to progress. A universal standard microprocessor bus has been proposed that has 8-bit bidirectional data lines, 6 power lines, a 16-bit bidirectional address bus, and 22 control lines. Some other buses now on the market are the Intel Multibus with 16-bit bidirectional data lines, a 16-bit address bus, 8 multilevel interrupt lines, 5 bus control arbitration lines, and several power and control lines. Some lines are three-state; other are open-collector (OR).

This section indicates briefly the degree of activity in the area of standardization, where new proposals occur almost daily.

8-7 SUMMARY

This chapter covers a multitude of special systems, including distributed systems, time-shared systems, a time-sharing language (sometimes used as an interractive compiler like FORTRAN), a system of control used by power companies, and concludes with a discussion of present micro-computer standard buses. This latter item is receiving considerable attention because at present no 16-bit standard bus has received total acceptance; thus, much more work is needed in this area.

9

Newer Devices

9-1 GENERAL

This chapter introduces the newer device interfaces associated with
microprocessors, including single-chip interfacing PCUs, standardization, fiber optics, and a description and comparison of different types
of control systems. The single-dip interfaces were introduced in Chapter 2. These were for microcomputers; typical interfaces for minicomputers were covered in Chapter 6. In Chapter 2 we introduced very
briefly the Motorola dips for their MC6800 and a tabulation of those
produced by Texas Instruments for their 990 series. The major differences are that minicomputers usually take a many-dip interface, while
microprocessors often use a single dip. Most of these new dips are
c-MOS LSIs but could also be m-MOS, H-MOS, I^2L, etc. For example,
UART, D/A, and A/D converters are often hybrids that combine a
variety of technologies. Among the devices described in this chapter
are two floppy disk controllers, a CRT controller, and an RS232C
interface.

9-2 SINGLE-CHIP AND MULTICHIP INTERFACES

Since a microprocessor may interface a variety of devices, all the interfacing dips can be mounted on a separate board, possibly along with the necessary RAM and ROM. But what must be pointed out is that each interface is potentially composed of a single dip. This is a decided improvement over those described in Chapter 6, and the process continues to improve steadily.

9-2.1 CRT Controllers

There are several CRT controllers on the market, each having varying degrees of power and other characteristics, and designed for special CRTs. For example, consider the diagram of the Motorola 6845 (Fig. 9-1). It generates a row count for the character generator. The signals for deflections [vertical (V) and horizontal (H)] start the (V) and (H) analog sweeps. These latter signals are really synching signals. Also provided is the blanking signal and a 14-bit address for the RAM buffer memory. The 6845 is equipped with a cursor register and a light-pen register which does not require a buffer. It can shift vertical lines across the screen or automatically display the next full screen of characters. Its programmable features include dot rasters per character, characters per line, lines per synch, horizontal and vertical synch positions, and use of the cursor for identification of a desired position on the screen.

9-2.2 A Floppy Disk Controller

National Electronics Corporation, among others, makes a one-chip floppy disk controller that will handle any disk formatting control with its I/O interface. It also directs the drive. Commands include write, read, read deleted data, read a track, scan (low, equal, or greater), write deleted data, format and track, move head track-to-track, recalibrate, sense interrupt status, sense drive status, specify. The basic system can operate from DIO or DMA. Figure 9-2 shows the chip connections.

Another example of a floppy disk controller is the FD1771, illustrated by Fig. 9-3. It contains all the lines and registers to complete the floppy disk microprocessor interface. The data shift register assembles 8 bits from the microprocessor data bus and puts it in or removes it from the serial-data floppy disk track. The data register is only a holding register to hold bytes during reading and writing operations. It communicates between the microprocessor data bus and the data out

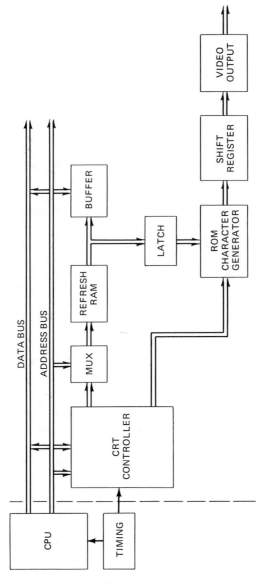

FIGURE 9-1 CRT dip block diagram.

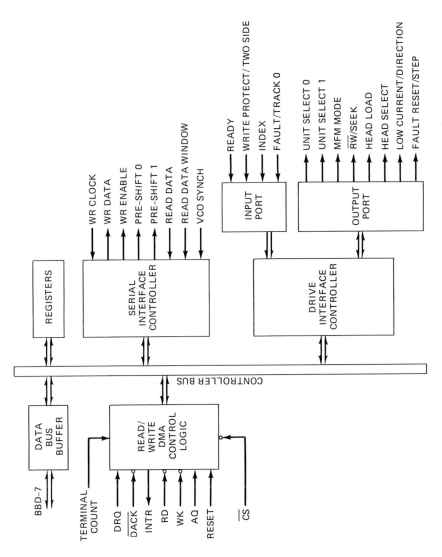

FIGURE 9-2 The NEC uPD765C floppy disk controller chip connections.

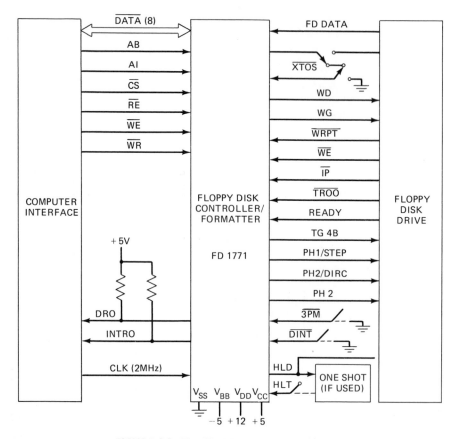

FIGURE 9-3 The FD1771 floppy disk controller.

buffer. The command register holds the 8-bit command being executed. The programmer loads this register to specify the disk operation. The sector register holds the address of the desired sector position. The track register holds the track number of the current head position. It is incremented or decremented up to 76 tracks on a regular-sized disk. Lastly, there is the status register, which holds status information of the controller.

9-2.3 Microprocessor to RS232C Interface

This process is often accomplished by applying a UART, as described in Chapter 1. The microprocessor output is usually ASC II code of 8-data bits, preceded by a start bit and followed by a parity bit and 1 or 2 stop bits. This is asynchronous transmitting/receiving insofar as UARTs are concerned, with serial transmitting/receiving. Control lines or strobes must be provided by additional dips for the micropro-

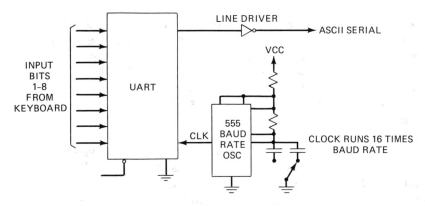

FIGURE 9-4 ASCII to RS232C interface.

cessor and RS232C interface. Figure 9-4 shows a keyboard/ASC II interface, using a UART, oscillator, and a line-driver.

9-3 STANDARDIZATION

The major problems existing at present are standardization of interfaces and software, especially for higher-level languages. Some of the interim standards are described in Chapters 2 and 8. All 16-bit devices can accommodate FORTRAN, BASIC, COBOL, and PASCAL. There are many other languages, but the interface problem for 16-bit devices has not as yet been standardized except in serial form, where RS232C, Mil. Std. 188, and Mil. Std. 13350 are the present standards except on high-speed links. Each 8-bit microprocessor either adheres to its own standard, or to IEEE Std. 488 (77), for 16-bit machines. The only one we know of is CAMAC, which is overly complex.

Standards are being proposed frequently, so the ultimate choice is still to be made.

9-4 FIBER OPTICS

Electromagnetic transmission either via wire or waveguides has a new competitor which is in an early stage of development; however, it has proved useful in a number of applications for both video and data transmission. We refer, of course, to fiber optics, where transmission is via a glass rod, the transmitter being an LED or other form of high-frequency source, and the receiver being a light-sensitive diode sometimes coded as PIN. Transmission rates have been achieved in excess of 20 MHz and for distances over 3 km. No doubt greater distance and higher frequencies will be realized in the future. The telephone companies are now transmitting multiplexed T-1 codes, and there are many potential uses for fiber optics transmission. Since it is totally free of electromagnetic interference, that makes it extremely useful in noisy electrical environments such as aircraft. In Las Vegas a 2.6 mile video link has been demonstrated. The T-1 code is shown in Fig. 9-5. Of course, Manchester or other codes could be employed. These systems have great potential for future communication systems of almost any length. Table 9-1 outlines the characteristics of some present systems.

A prototype fiber optics system was first used in the 1950s. Traveling upward through a transparent capstan, light passed through holes in a paper tape and then upward through plastic tubes about 5 in. long to eight photomultiplier tubes (very bulky devices) so as to read the eight holes in parallel on the tape in a crosswise direction. The narrowness of the tape and the 1 in. diameter of each photomultiplier tube required such a method. Today, direct current exceeding 400 MHz travels up to several miles via thin glass or plastic fibers, which act like waveguides in that different frequencies follow different paths and thus can be separated at the far end for the individual messages transmitted. Several message paths are included in a single strand.

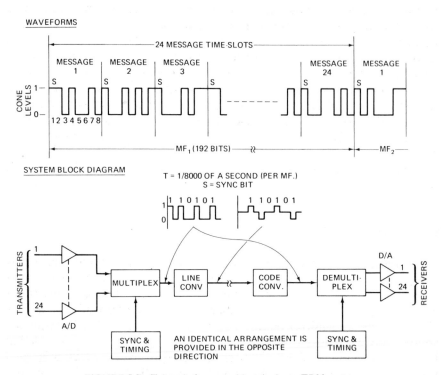

FIGURE 9-5 T-1 code form used in telephone TDM systems.

TABLE 9-1

CHARACTERISTICS OF FIBER OPTICS LINKS

1. *Links in this country are approaching 5 miles in length without repeaters.*
2. *Japan has reported a link of 50 km without repeaters.*
3. *Transmissions exceeding 600 megabits per second is approaching.*
4. *Electrical noise rejection is unsurpassed. Thus, links can be used in severe electrical noise environments.*
5. *Up to 16 separate strands have been used in one cable.*
6. *The noise protection level is 5 db or greater.*
7. *Mean-time-between-failures (MTBF), a common measure of reliability, is greater than 60,000 hr.*
8. *The types of transmitting and receiving diodes, their intensity or sensitivity, the material of the path, the types and numbers of junctions, the number of ports, and the bandwidths are all important aspects of the path's capability.*

Glass strands are often favored, since the attenuation (in decibels per kilometer) is very low (being about 6 dB for a bandwidth of 400 MHz). Usually, about 10 separate strands are wound about a steel cable, which increases strength and avoids possible strand breakage. Repair of broken glass strands is difficult so, in some cases, plastics are favored, which are easier to butt together and to repair than glass; however, attenuation is usually greater. Strands can be coated to reduce loss, and sharp bends should be avoided. As to data formats, usually T-1 or Manchester codes are preferred, and the RS232C interface or simple TTL circuits can be provided. Repeaters are usually furnished for long cable lengths, but narrowing the bandwidth or using more powerful transmitters or more sensitive receivers can help. For unusual circumstances, special strands have been developed to reduce attenuation. Transmitters, receivers, and the optic path are the main components of a fiber optics system. One company sells a cabinet that can hold to 16 of any of the above components, the cabinet dimensions being 8.8 in. high, 19 in. wide, and 12.9 in. deep. Including the power supply equipment, it weighs 151 lb.

Fiber optics links have many applications in addition to telephone messages in digitized form. Such applications include telemetry and links in noisy electrical environments such as railroad yards or aircraft. In one instance fiber optics was considered for the Space Shuttle program. Figure 9-6 shows a typical cable cross section.

In reality, the science of fiber optics is now emerging from the laboratory, but many interesting experiments are proving that it has real promise, thus complementing the use of wire cables and waveguides, with some advantages that neither possesses. Figure 9-7 is an example of a transmitter and receiver of a fiber optics link.

In 1980, there has been a great extension in the use of fiber optics

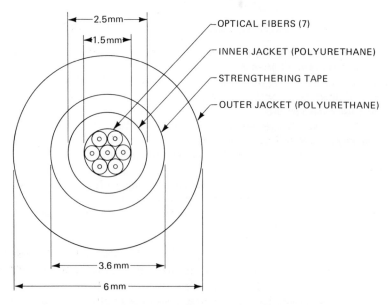

FIGURE 9-6 Fiber optics cable cross section.

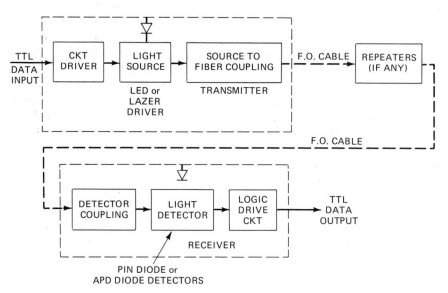

FIGURE 9-7 Block diagram of a transmitter and receiver of a fiber optic link.

links. In Japan one link exceeds 26 miles in length. Many new links in this country and Canada can now transmit data approximately 9 miles without requiring repeaters. This technique is spreading rapidly.

9-5 VIDEO DISKS

A technique for recording color television has a potentially large bulk-store device, and many laboratories are examining laser excited and read disks for digital bulk-store usefulness. At present, several Japanese manufacturers have converted color TV pictures to a digital form and store these for immediate playback. The same technique can be used for storing data. The disk material is silicon and the lazer records separate patterns for "1s" and "0s". The packing density is extremely close, and many millions of bits can be stored on a single disk. The density is greater than magnetic recording, permanent, and potentially inexpensive. These devices are still in the developmental stage, and standards could easily change. It will be interesting to observe the comparative progress of CCD and magnetic bubble memories. Figure 9-8 shows a video disk system in its fundamental form. The major problem with video disks is that it is difficult to record over previously recorded data and erase what was formerly recorded. This is why research is still proceeding, as well as attempting denser recording for those applications where erasing is not a requirement.

9-6 ADVANCED TRENDS

9-6.1 General

There are basically four types of control logic:

- Analog control (ADC)
- Supervisory control (SDC)
- Digital direct control (DDC)
- Distributed control (DC)

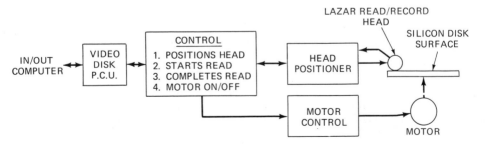

FIGURE 9-8 The fundamental working of a video disk.

All of these are described briefly, with accompanying figures. These terms at the system level have been used for years, but their significance has increased with the advent of the microcomputer.

9-6.2 Analog Control System

Analog control is used only in those plants where the operation is simple, although such systems generally increase efficiency at least 10%. They are both easy to run and understand. One personally adjusts test parameters. If such systems are connected together via a supervision system, the supervisor program must be written, as well as operational routines, troubleshooting, editing programs, etc. See Fig. 9-9.

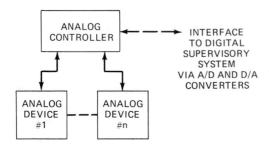

FIGURE 9-9 Analog control system.

9-6.3 Supervisory Control System

This is an analog control system, but with the added features of controlling and providing programs to, or data to or from, several computers. Supervisory control has found wide acceptance to control large, complex systems. See Fig. 9-10 for a typical example.

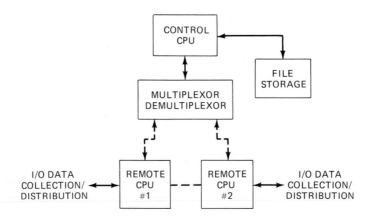

FIGURE 9-10 Supervisory control system.

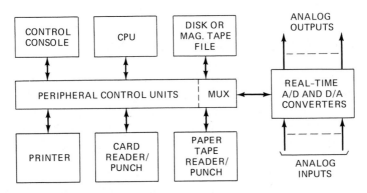

FIGURE 9-11 Digital direct control block diagram.

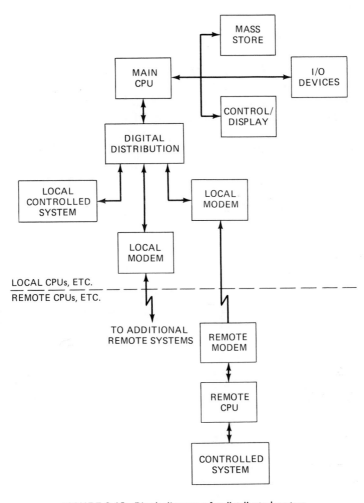

FIGURE 9-12 Block diagram of a distributed system.

9-6.4   Digital Direct Control System (DDC)

This system uses all-digital logic. Any analog inputs or outputs are provided by multiplexers, A/D converters, D/A converters, etc. Most often, the inputs and outputs are digital, either serial or parallel. These systems were introduced during the 1960s, but with the advent of the microcomputer their power has increased dramatically. Much processing is done at the main computer station, but DDC can have many characteristics of distributed systems. Usually, there are many associated peripherals for sensing, printing out results, and placing data on disks, paper tape, or magnetic tape. See Fig. 9-11 for a typical diagram of this system.

9-6.5   Distributed Control System

This system has many peripheral computers reporting to a main computer. It also commands the peripheral computers, providing them with programs, evaluates status, gathers data, and stores. Having many peripherals, when such a system is used cross-country, it is called a *time-share system*. This does not mean that a single plant may not operate other computers; such multicomputer operation is actually a common occurrence. With the advent of the 16-bit microcomputer, this means that the former controller processor can also be a microcomputer, or a minicomputer, if so desired. See Fig. 9-12 for a diagram of a distributed system.

9-7   SUMMARY

Section 9-2 describes a few single-chip interfaces, primarily for microcomputer use. However, these cards can hold several chips, including some ROM or RAM additional memories. Most manufacturers of microcomputers supply these chips for their own products. Section 9-3 briefly summarizes the problems of standardization. Those discussed in Chapter 2 are approach standards for Motorola or Texas Instruments computers, but those listed in Chapter 8 depend on the bus type used, none of which are universal industry standards. Section 9-4 explains fiber optics, a rapidly developing phenomenon in communications. Section 9-5 covers briefly the new video disk form of bulk-store. Section 9-6 characterizes various forms of computer systems and attempts to define them.

Designing
Computer-based
Systems

10-1 COMPUTER SYSTEMS

10-1.1 General

Designing an efficient computer system requires substantial exper-
tise and resources. First, there is the task of defining exactly what the
system must accomplish. What additional tasks must be anticipated for
the future? A study must be made of hardware equipment and software required, and where it is to come from. What are the necessary
peripherals? Here a definite comparative study must be accomplished,
noting what is available, from whom, prices, and software. Once the
likely processor is determined, the available peripherals, their usefulness, and efficiency must be evaluated as a whole, since they apply to
the system under consideration. This process is a real team effort because numerous variables must be resolved. Another consideration:
now there is a possible new approach to programming, called *firmware*.
Will this eliminate some of the new software preparation?
  Add to these factors the proliferation of possible memory types

for main store (running from cores and RAMs to magnetic bubbles) and the vast array of peripherals (including highly intelligent terminals) exerts great pressure on a design team to make optimum selections. This chapter covers some of the recent developments.

10-1.2 Distinctions between Mainframes, Minicomputers, and Microcomputers

Actual distinctions between a mainframe versus mini- and micro-computers have blurred. When using a digital computer for an analog system, there will be an operator's control panel, an operating system, hardware arithmetic, a processor [the latter two are generally lumped as an arithmetic logic unit (ALU)], internal memory RAM and ROM, a software package, mass storage, aquisition devices, printers, actuators, etc. The latter four classes require a PCU to make them compatible with the processor. These are a sampling of the features that must be resolved by a design team.

The distinction today between processor classes depends on (1) word length and (2) cost. Microcomputers vary in cost from a little over $100 to a few thousand. They presently have word lengths up to 16 bits. The overlapping minicomputers cost up to $50,000 and have word lengths up to 32 bits. Most costly are the mainframes, priced up to $1,000,000 and having up to 64-bit word lengths.

Computer systems are now found in every aspect of business and control (missiles, aircraft, automobiles, manufacturing, power systems, temperature control, etc.). Other important uses are entertainment devices and home devices, as well as communications. Regardless of the application, the system design is vital. For example, airport traffic control is a difficult problem. A special processing system has been proposed, that of an array processor. As visualized, this equipment would keep track of literally hundreds of aircraft by utilization of a processor with hundreds of ALUs. This type of machine was built years ago at the University of Illinois and was called *ILLIAC*.

Although such special situations arise from time to time, still the usual tradeoff involves reasonably conventional mainframes, minicomputers, microcomputers, their peripherals, and their memory concepts. In other cases a dedicated controller may be the best approach, thus avoiding a computer entirely. A common determination is often between a mainframe and a multiprocessor system, where a central minicomputer communicates with microcomputers located at the points of operation. The microcomputers do the main control work, while the minicomputer provides central programs communicated to the microcomputers, and has the main record peripherals under its personal control.

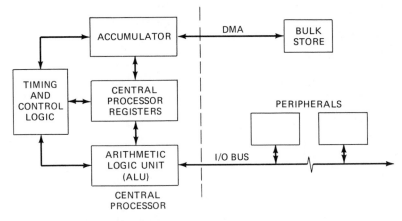

FIGURE 10-1 Conventional computer.

10-2 CENTRAL PROCESSING UNIT

Word length, length of time to access memory, and an individual register's characteristics are the main features of an ALU. Other things are important, too; for example, consider the *add* time and the interrupt system. Longer words mean larger numbers and thus greater capability of a single instruction—such as more than a single address. A conventional computer diagram is shown in more detail in Fig. 10-1, as compared to the basic figure shown in Chapter 1, although individual registers are not indicated. A second form of dedicated computer is shown in Fig. 10-2. This form of design is oriented about its internal registers for a specific application and appears much like an Interdata 7/16 or an Intel 8080A. The organization of Fig. 10-3 manipulates its

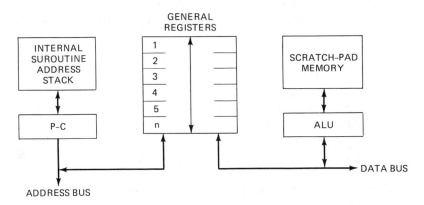

FIGURE 10-2 Dedicated applications-register oriented.

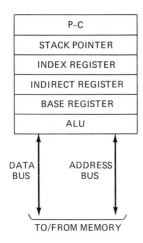

| P–C |
| STACK POINTER |
| INDEX REGISTER |
| INDIRECT REGISTER |
| BASE REGISTER |
| ALU |

DATA BUS   ADDRESS BUS

TO/FROM MEMORY   **FIGURE 10-3** General applications-memory oriented.

data in and out of memory space, as in many of the mainframes as well as in many of the newer microcomputers such as Texas Instruments' Series TMS990. Because of manipulation many registers are required to keep track of the data. In general, the more registers, the more flexible the central processor.

There are three basic operations required of any computer:

1. Move data between registers, memory, and I/O.
2. Perform logic control for itself and the rest of the system.
3. Perform logic and arithmetic actions on data.

Usually, there are five general types of instructions:

1. *Data transfer:* These move data between registers and memory.
2. *Branching:* These cause conditional and unconditional "jumping", providing program looping and calling or return from subroutines.
3. *I/O stack and interrupt control:* These manipulate stacks, control I/O ports, and alter internal control flags.
4. *Arithmetic operations:* These include addition, subtraction, comparing, division, multiplication (on either fixed-point or floating-point data), and complements.
5. *Logical operations:* These include ANDing, ORing, exclusive-ORing, etc., as well as shifting or rotating data.

Various computers may classify their instructions differently. Register addressing is inherent and does not cause concern for an operator. However, memory addressing is something else again. For example, the simplest way to execute a program is to enter the first address of the program counter. Its contents are transferred to the MAR, and the instruction or data appears at the MBR. This technique is known as *direct addressing*, which depends on the program counter being incremented each time. *Indirect addressing* may also be done. In this case the program counter (P-C) calls a word whose contents is considered a new address to be executed. This technique extends the capability to address more words normally out of range of the original address bits of the original word called. A third approach is to modify the original address by adding to it a value stored in an index register, all done in the accumulator. This technique is quite common for branching instructions. All of these methods permit short instructions to simulate mainframe instructions with their added power.

In general, the following generalizations apply:

1. Long word lengths permit more powerful and versatile instructions.

2. Instruction set size of itself is not a conclusive factor; rather, how set size applies to the job to be done is more important, and thus, this factor may require a study of the operations to be performed versus the instruction set.

3. In the same manner as (2) above, cycle speed must be considered and its effect analyzed versus the task at hand.

Because of the wide differences that now exist between presently available processors, a study of their characteristics versus their anticipated tasks is mandatory to obtain the best match. In addition to those items listed above, the register count, the number of accumulators, and the form of interrupts should also be considered. With several accumulators, several instructions can probably be executed simultaneously, this feature could be important for solutions to some special problems. Thus, the selection of computer architecture is not a trivial task. Table 10-1 lists some of the differences that presently exist.

10-3 MAIN STORAGE

10-3.1 Basic Types

As to memories that are internal to the processor (core, RAM, ROM, etc.) and external to the processor (bulk-store, CCD, bubbles, and rotating disks), there is a strong possibility in the future of CCD and magnetic bubbles replacing the present internal memories, particularly for special applications. So far we have classified these as periph-

TABLE 10-1

TYPICAL PROCESSORS NOT INCLUDED IN TABLE 2-1

Manufacturer	Motorola	Intel	Zilog	American Micro-Devices	Honeywell
Model	MC68000	8086	Z8002	AM2900*	HDC5301*
Material	H-MOS	n-MOS	n-MOS	TTL, Schottky, or c-MOS	TTL, Schottky, or c-MOS
Data bits	16	16	16	16	16
Memory bus	16	16	16	16	16
Instructions	61	133	207	Depends on ROM setting	96
Package pins (μ-processor) chip	60	40	40	40	40
Add time (μsec)	1.0	2.5	2.0	1.0	1.0
Memory cycle (nsec)	150	200	250	200	200
Interrupts	165	256	—	20	20

*These bit-slice processors are described in Section 2-2 and Fig. 2-13.

erals because thus far that is how they have been used for the most part. Magnetic tapes, disks, floppies, cassettes, etc., are also in that category.

There are some disadvantages in using CCD or magnetic bubbles alone as main memory: since they work in serialized loops, they are slower than RAM or ROM and also more expensive per bit. Within a year or two access time will be 35 to 40 nanosec for n-MOS devices, and a newer, faster, denser H-MOS is now approaching bipolar speeds. As for CCD and magnetic bubbles, their density will also increase, speeds will increase, and their cost will decrease. At the present time, CCD and magnetic bubbles are used as a cache memory tied into the system between its main memory and long access-time disks, cassettes, tapes, etc. These cache memories are loaded from/to the rotating bulk-stores while the main program is being executed. This process expedites access to externally stored data by main memory.

10-3.2 Static Memories

These were covered generally in Sections 4-4 and 4-5, but here we are viewing the possible replacement of RAM and ROM of main memory by CCD or magnetic bubbles.

10-3.3 Dynamic Memories

These are the magnetic tapes, disk files (magnetic cores, floppies, and silicon disks). Figure 10-4 illustrates the projected rise in density of magnetic disk recording. Table 10-3 lists some of the aspects of

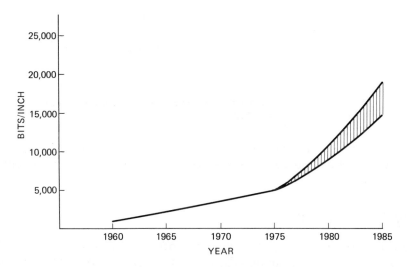

FIGURE 10-4 Trends in density of disk storage.

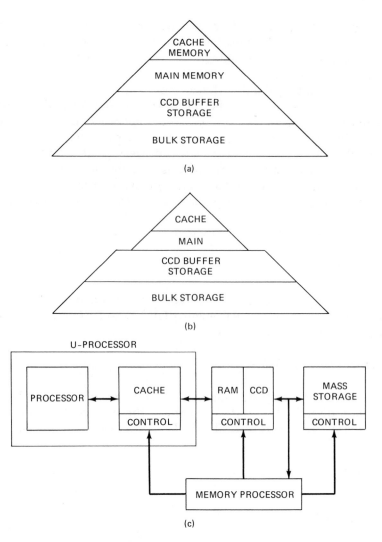

FIGURE 10-5 Development of distributed control of a processor memory.
(a) mid-1970's, (b) late 1970's, (c) probable future trends.

moving media storage. Figure 10-5 shows a possible hierarchy of a microcomputer memory system. Here the processor itself controls the memory.

10-4 FIRMWARE

Firmware is a leading challenger to software. Firmware is basically a ROM memory that can be substituted to change a program. The object is to reduce operational expense, since software cost is the largest part

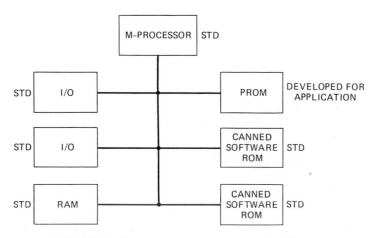

FIGURE 10-6 Future μ-processor system standard firmware.

of the initial expense of a new system and its cost remains virtually constant. Conversely, ePROM memory chips are decreasing in cost rapidly. The basic problem with firmware chips is that what can be put on them can also be read off; thus, it could be that programs would be easier to steal.

However, the prospects for firmware are promising. The military is rapidly implementing use of the compiler PASCAL, which is a standard programming method. Thus, in the future, the use of standard software and firmware modules is a probability. One could visualize (as shown in Fig. 10-6) a processor comprised entirely of firmware—all standard chips for programming and interfacing. Texas Instruments and Motorola are pioneers in this approach and have demonstrated the feasibility of replacing software by hardware.

Only one special firmware chip is required to control programming; otherwise, memory and interface chips are all standard firmware. The chip to control programming is also a firmware chip.

10-5 PERIPHERALS

In regard to peripherals we shall cover here the many advances in the area of magnetic coatings for special cartridges, floppy disks, and cassettes. These, coupled with CCDs, magnetic bubbles, and silicon disks, as well as the use of electronic beams now undergoing laboratory research, will probably be intermediate between disks, floppies, and mainframe ROM and RAM memories. A floppy in one system has been accelerated and connects to main memory via fixed heads and a DMA channel; there are four disks in this setup. Achievable density in this system is 12,000 bits/in. Table 10-2 lists anticipated future disk

TABLE 10-2

FUTURE DISK IMPROVEMENTS

1. *Closer tracks*
2. *Higher bit densities on a per-bit basis*
3. *Higher reliability of electrical and mechanical parts*
4. *Higher degree of reliability for recording and readback*
5. *Less electrical noise to intermingle with data-causing errors*
6. *Newer techniques, such as video disks, over which new data can be recorded, erasing old recordings in the process*
7. *Lower cost for equipment*
8. *More available combinations of floppies and disks (that is, Winchester drives)*

improvements, extrapolated from 1980 systems, and Table 10-3 lists access times, as well as the capacities of various storage mediums. Figure 10-7 shows floppy disk system architecture.

It is anticipated that Table 10-4, by 1981, will have traced the bits/inch and tracks/inch over two decades.

In summary, where the typical access for floppies is 200 to 500 millisec, bubble memories can be accessed in 4 to 7 millisec, and CCDs

TABLE 10-3

DISK IMPROVEMENTS AFTER 1978—EXTRAPOLATED

1. *Double the 1978 bit density by 1985.*
2. *Double the 1978 track density by 1985.*
3. *The video disk should be available for computers by 1983. Its storage density should quadruple by 1985. At present, research is being accomplished on reading over pre-written data causing the old data to be erased.*
4. *Improved methods for writing of previously stored data should be available.*
5. *Since these disks are paralleling the development of television recording methods, fallout from this development should be of assistance.*
6. *Although presently available, the next few years should see great competitive improvements as well as improvements in both CCD and magnetic bubble memories. In 1980, magnetic bubble memories are readily available in 1 megabyte units from a number of suppliers. The same is true of CCDs.*

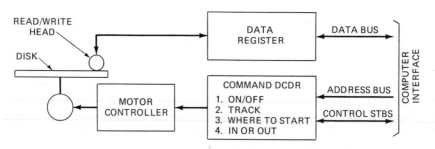

FIGURE 10-7 Floppy disk architecture.

TABLE 10-4

BIT AND TRACK DENSITIES (1960–1985)

Bit density,	500 bpi	Tracks,	10/in.	(1960)
Bit density,	1000 bpi	Tracks,	20/in.	(1965)
Bit density,	1600 bpi	Tracks,	30/in.	(1970)
Bit density,	3200 bpi	Tracks,	40/in.	(1975)
Bit density,	6400 bpi	Tracks,	60-80/in.	(1980)
Bit density,	10000 bpi	Tracks,	100/in.	(1985)

Note: bpi = bits per inch along the track.

have selectable data transfer rates of 1 to 3 megabytes/sec and access times approaching 0.7 millisec.

10-6 TERMINALS

Terminals have been developed intensively since the introduction of Teletype equipment. Today, a terminal is more likely to be a CRT, along with devices to process permanent records such as card equipment, paper tape equipment, printers/plotters, cassettes, floppies, and magnetic tape. The modern concept of distributed processing accommodates stand-alone terminals comprised of as many of the above devices as needed, and frees a host computer for handling graphics. With a computer at each terminal many devices may operate independently or through the system peripherals often concentrated at the location of the host computer, thus providing a versatile and powerful organization of equipment.

Figure 10-7 shows the architecture of a floppy disk memory. The device must be addressed to provide a transfer of data in serial groups of words or bytes. There must be a control decoder to cause the device to function and to control the flow of data in or out. Since the computer output may be parallel, a shift register internal to the floppy disk's logic would be required. The number of words to be transferred must be stored either internally to the floppy disk or via DMA. If a serial transfer is available from the computer, it would be possible, but not likely, to eliminate the shift register because of the differences in computer/floppy disk normal data flow speeds. Thus, data to be transferred and data addresses must be supplied from the computer.

As for computer displays there are four basic types: data representations, line drawings, imagery, and graphics. Data representation is normally in the form of alphanumerics but can also be shown as plots or bar graphs substituting for tabulations. By using colors, a third dimension (such as heat intensity) can be displayed, along with its distribution as an X-Y or logarithmic plot.

Line drawings are derived from schematics, maps, mechanical or architectural drawings and, with color, can be three dimensional; the other two coordinates are naturally X and Y.

Imagery involves pictures, such as photographs, but can also accommodate superposition of other information on the pictures, including alphanumerics and graphs. For example, TV contains over 70,000 dots, whereas an imagery display may exceed over 300,000 dots.

Graphics often superimpose alphanumeric text on graphic data, transmitted via ASC II code. A very popular use of this type of display is employed in editing text displayed on a CRT. Words can be added, deleted, and paragraphs can be repositioned. Many CRT displays use the raster-scan technique of TV, but in the memory all data (alphanumeric, graphic, and imagery) must be stored. Memory storage can be extensive since a dot is needed for each bit and color location.

When the final display has been corrected and placed in storage, it is often output on a printer/plotter for a permanent record. Developments continue at a rapid pace in all of these areas.

For software control many display generators decode and process high-level, binary-formatted instruction sets transmitted over a 16-bit interface. The instruction sets are executed and/or stored as subprograms in the host computer for deferred execution. The system designers load the control code for display processor control, refine the instruction set, or implement their operational functions.

As to graphic advances, real-time generators are available. The instruction set addresses 32 × 32K coordinates. Picture magnification is accomplished by internal coordinate transformations, where line thickness, texture, and character size are not affected. If the host computer is not used to scale, this is done over the 16-bit bus, where the capability of eight displays is built into the system.

Often, clustering of the terminals centralizes the distribution of intelligence and is a function of high-speed data communication networks. However, up to 70% more software is required for clustering: hence, firmware is often substituted.

Vector generation runs at control speed—proportional to the vector length. The difference between vector speeds and the dot matrix approach is attributed to the bit microprocessor. The microprocessor 16-bit design or architecture allows the system designer to increase throughput with microcoded floating-point instructions including those for floating-point arithmetic.

Character generation, as opposed to vector generation, is the simplest and most cost-effective approach to CRT graphics. Normally, a character generator requires a minimum of software development and hardware support. The CRT controller chip provides the required timing and control pulses for the character generator, memory, and CRT monitor. Figure 10-8 shows a simplified diagram of a character genera-

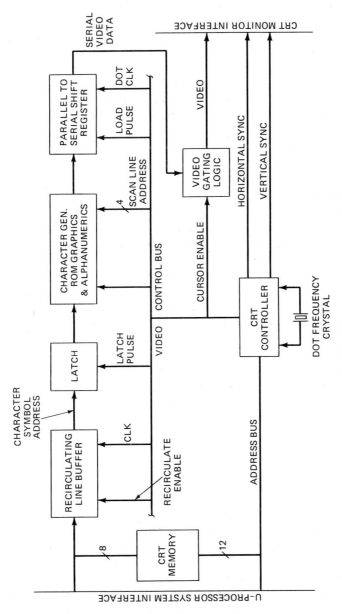

FIGURE 10-8 Character generator graphics.

tor that uses a microprocessor as a CRT controller. The operation is enhanced by replacing a circulating line buffer between the CRT memory and character generator. This configuration allows the system controller to access memory on all but one scan line.

With this system's graphics capabilities it is not possible to generate individual dots; only character cells are available. However, formats like circuit schematics and bar graphs can be combined with alphanumerics.

The character generator's address for a character can be loaded serially, and the character buffer is modified by placing a line buffer between the CRT memory and the generator. A shift register on the scan line is loaded before the first video line of the character row. These addresses are then recirculated one row line less than the number of scan lines per character row. This system is very attractive if there is heavy access to CRT memory.

If a high resolution system is needed every dot on the CRT may be individually controlled and must be mapped as a specific memory CRT data bit, whereas separate alphanumeric characters or symbols may be separately stored. In this case the higher-order data bits from the CRT memory define whether the lower-order bits are graphics, video data, ASC II, or another data or symbol code.

Dumb terminals have replaced data printers because they can be edited easily. The intelligence for these terminals is built into their logic or the computer program. This type of terminal cannot by itself print hard copy.

Intelligence terminals benefit from distributed systems, and can benefit from any of several printing methods, such as thermal or impact printing matrices. Some intelligence printers are operated from a dual data base, which depends on ROM expansion; this allows the system designers to program terminals for automatic spacing of CRT dumps. This approach can control data to and from plotters and printers, etc.

10-7 SUMMARY

This chapter discusses modern computer design. It distinguishes between mainframes, minicomputers, and microcomputers. Even though the entire field is merging rapidly, it is important to recognize the various levels of computers and how they relate to distributed systems—a fast-growing branch of computer science. Some of the rapid changes of memory types and the direction of their development, bulk-store advances and projections are provided, as well as advances that are continuing in the display area. Terminals, peripherals, and a new topic, firmware, are introduced. Our intention is to indicate that computer advances are continuing at so rapid a pace as to render present knowledge as transitory.

Appendix

Number Systems

A-1 GENERAL

In the Western world we use the decimal number system, and we think in terms of the numbers 0 to 9. But reflecting for a moment, what does the number 897 really represent? It means, simply, 7 + 90 + 800, or, written another way,

$$8 \times 10^2 + 9 \times 10^1 + 7 \times 10^0 = 897$$

The digits 8, 9, and 7 are called *coefficients*, and the digits 0, 1, 2 are the *exponents* of the base 10 number system (the decimal system). Of course, other bases can be used, but usually only for very special applications.

First, we will consider the binary system, where there are only two coefficients, "1" and "0". The base is 2, so numbers are written as 1000111, which means, going from right to left:

$$1 \times 2^6 + 0 \times 2^5 + 0 \times 2^4 + 0 \times 2^3 + 1 \times 2^2 + 1 \times 2^1 + 1 \times 2^0$$

Now,

$$2^6 = 64, \, 2^5 = 32, \, 2^4 = 16, \, 2^3 = 8, \, 2^2 = 4, \, 2^1 = 2, \, 2^0 = 1, \text{ etc.}$$

Thus, the binary number represented totals $64 + 4 + 2 + 1 = 71$ in decimal notation. Binary numbers are of special interest because computers are designed to work with binary quantities or codes comprising binary quantities. Computer gates deal exclusively with codes of "1s" and "0s".

A-2 BINARY NUMBER SYSTEM

Binary numbers are listed in tabular form in Table A-1. Note that positive numbers usually have a "0" to the left of the binary point, and

TABLE A-1

Number value	Sign magnitude*	2s complement
15	0.001111	0.001111
14	0.001110	0.001110
13	0.001101	0.001101
12	0.001100	0.001100
11	0.001011	0.001011
10	0.001010	0.001010
9	0.001001	0.001001
8	0.001000	0.001000
7	0.000111	0.000111
6	0.000110	0.000110
5	0.000101	0.000101
4	0.000100	0.000100
3	0.000011	0.000011
2	0.000010	0.000010
1	0.000001	0.000001
0	0.000000	0.000000
−1	1.000001	1.111111
−2	1.000010	1.111110
−3	1.000011	1.111101
−4	1.000100	1.111100
−5	1.000101	1.111011
•	•	•
•	•	•
−15	1.001111	1.110001
etc.	etc.	etc.

*By the notation employed, the numbers really represented are $n \times (2^{-6})$, where n is the number value in the left column. xxxxxx represents 2^{-6}.

negative numbers have a "1". The reader is referred to any book on digital computers or logic for a complete discussion of binary arithmetic operation details.*

As mentioned, in the binary number system the binary point is usually at the left-hand side of the number, with a "0" or "1" preceding it; this is done primarily to ease arithmetic operations and conversions. A positive number is preceded by a "0", and a negative number preceded by a "1". The remainder of the number to the right of the binary point is in complement form for negative numbers. To find the complement of any number in binary form, reverse "1s" and "0s", and add a "1" to the extreme right-hand column. Thus, the complement of 11011 is:

$$11111 - 11011 = 00100 + 00001 = 00101$$

The complement of any number is obtained by subtracting it from its base and adding a 1 to the LSD. This is defined as the *true* complement. It may be checked by adding the number to its complement, and the result would be zero. For example, $11011 + 00101 = 00000$. Generally, complements in any number system are found by the same method. The main advantage of complements to computer hardware is that subtraction can be done by adding the minuend to the complement of the subtrahend. Thus, a computer need only be programmed on how to add, since multiplications are formed by multiple summing and shifting, and division by multiple subtractions and shifting.

Conversions between binary, octal, and hexadecimal systems are easy; they can be done by visual inspection and partitioning. For example, binary 100101101010 is hexadecimal (HD) 96A, which is determined by sectoring: $1001 = 9$, $0110 = 6$, $1010 = A$. For the octal conversion, binary is sectored into groups of three bits, which means that the above binary is 4552 in the octal system. For conversions in reverse, the digits are replaced by their binary equivalents. Conversion from decimal to binary is not as straightforward. One must continually divide a number by 2 and note the remainders. Arranging the digits last to first, one obtains the binary equivalent. For binary to decimal conversion, add the powers of 2 equivalents, and sum for the decimal total. Octal and HD conversions are covered in Sections A-3, A-4, and A-5.

Tables A-2 and A-3 are shown to assist in octal operations of addition and subtraction; Tables A-4 and A-5 are included to assist in HD operations of addition and subtraction.

*Deem, Muchow, Zeppa, Digital Computer Circuits and Concepts, 2nd Ed., Reston Publishing Company Inc., Reston, Va., 1977.
Eadie, D, Minicomputers: Theory and Operation, Reston Publishing Company Inc., Reston, Va., 1979.

A-3 OCTAL NUMBER SYSTEMS

Octal notation is derived from a 3-bit binary code. The relationship of the binary and octal codes is represented by the following listing. Octal digits include 0, 1, 2, 3, 4, 5, 6, and 7.

Octal	Binary		Octal	Binary
0	000		4	100
1	001		5	101
2	010		6	110
3	011		7	111

A-3.1 Octal Addition and Subtraction

```
 1   |    1   |
     |  7  4  |  5
     |  2  2  |  5
     |--------|-----
     |  9  7  | 12
     | - 8    | - 8
     |--------|-----
 1   |  1  7  |  4   (sum)
```

```
 1   |    5   | 13
 2   | 10  6  | 13
 1   |  7  0  |  7
     |--------|-----
     |  1  5  |  6   (remainder)
```

TABLE A-2

OCTAL ADDITION

	1	2	3	4	5	6	7
1	2	3	4	5	6	7	10
2	3	4	5	6	7	10	11
3	4	5	6	7	10	11	12
4	5	6	7	10	11	12	13
5	6	7	10	11	12	13	14
6	7	10	11	12	13	14	15
7	10	11	12	13	14	15	16

TABLE A-3

OCTAL MULTIPLICATION

	1	2	3	4	5	6	7
1	1	2	3	4	5	6	7
2	2	4	6	10	12	14	16
3	3	6	11	14	17	22	25
4	4	10	14	20	24	30	34
5	5	12	17	24	31	40	43
6	6	14	22	30	40	44	52
7	7	16	25	34	43	52	61

A-3.2 Octal Multiplication

```
              3  6  5
              2  1  3
            ----------
         1  1  2  7
            2  1
         ----------
         1  3  3  7   X3
         3  6  5      X1
         ----------
         5  2  0  7
      6  4  2         X2
      ----------
         9  4  0  7
      6  9  4  0  7
```

Octal system digits use 3 bits and include the digits from 0 to 7. HD systems use 4 bits and include the digits and letters 0, 1, 2, 3, 4, 5, 6, 7, 8, 9, A, B, C, D, E, and F.

HD	Octal	HD	Octal
0	0000	8	1000
1	0001	9	1001
2	0010	A	1010
3	0011	B	1011
4	0100	C	1100
5	0101	D	1101
6	0110	E	1110
7	0111	F	1111

A-4.1 HD Addition and Subtraction

```
F C A 5                    9 →16 ⎫
1 A 2 B          F  C  A  5 ⎬ = 21
                 1  A  2  B ⎭
  0 6 C 0        
1 1 0 1          E  2  7  A  (remainder)
                 
1 1 6 D 0  (sum)
```

The subtraction problem could have been worked by converting 1A2B to the twos complement and adding. To convert to twos complement, subtract 1A2B from FFFF and add 1 to the LSB.

```
F F F F
1 A 2 B

E 5 D 4
      1

E 5 D 5  (complement 1A2B)
```

A-4.2 HD Multiplication

```
   36F        36F        36F        36F         36F
 X BE2       X 2        X E        X B        X BE2

   6CE        A42        125        6DE ←
   1          25D        24A        3012 ←
              
   6DE        2F12       1       ┌→ 26C5
                         26C5 ──┘  29CBFE
              1
              
              3012
```

HD ADDITION

	1	2	3	4	5	6	7	8	9	A	B	C	D	E	F
1	2	3	4	5	6	7	8	9	A	B	C	D	E	F	10
2	3	4	5	6	7	8	9	A	B	C	D	E	F	10	11
3	4	5	6	7	8	9	A	B	C	D	E	F	10	11	12
4	5	6	7	8	9	A	B	C	D	E	F	10	11	12	13
5	6	7	8	9	A	B	C	D	E	F	10	11	12	13	14
6	7	8	9	A	B	C	D	E	F	10	11	12	13	14	15
7	8	9	A	B	C	D	E	F	10	11	12	13	14	15	16
8	9	A	B	C	D	E	F	10	11	12	13	14	15	16	17
9	A	B	C	D	E	F	10	11	12	13	14	15	16	17	18
A	B	C	D	E	F	10	11	12	13	14	15	16	17	18	19
B	C	D	E	F	10	11	12	13	14	15	16	17	18	19	1A
C	D	E	F	10	11	12	13	14	15	16	17	18	19	1A	1B
D	E	F	10	11	12	13	14	15	16	17	18	19	1A	1B	1C
E	F	10	11	12	13	14	15	16	17	18	19	1A	1B	1C	1D
F	10	11	12	13	14	15	16	17	18	19	1A	1B	1C	1D	1E

A-5 CONVERSIONS

HD to decimal example (E62):

$$E = 14 \times 16 = 224$$
$$\text{Add 6:} \quad \underline{+ 6}$$
$$230 \times 16 = 3680$$
$$\text{Add 2:} \quad \underline{+ 2}$$
$$3682 _{(10)}$$

Decimal to HD:

	Remainder
16) 3628	
16) 230	2
14	6
	E

Since 14 = E   Therefore, $3682_{(10)} = E62_{(HD)}$

HD MULTIPLICATION

	1	2	3	4	5	6	7	8	9	A	B	C	D	E	F
1	1	2	3	4	5	6	7	8	9	A	B	C	D	E	F
2	2	4	6	8	A	C	E	10	12	14	16	18	1A	1C	1E
3	3	6	9	C	F	12	15	18	1B	1E	21	24	27	2A	2D
4	4	8	C	10	14	18	1C	20	24	28	2C	30	34	38	3C
5	5	A	F	14	19	1E	23	28	2D	32	37	3C	41	46	4B
6	6	C	12	18	1E	24	2A	30	36	3C	42	48	4E	54	5A
7	7	E	15	1C	23	2A	31	38	3F	46	4D	54	5B	62	69
8	8	10	18	20	28	30	38	40	48	50	58	60	68	70	78
9	9	12	1B	24	2D	36	3F	48	51	5A	63	6C	75	7E	87
A	A	14	1E	28	32	3C	46	50	5A	64	6E	78	82	8C	96
B	B	16	21	2C	37	42	4D	58	63	6E	79	84	8F	9A	A5
C	C	18	24	30	3C	48	54	60	6C	78	84	90	9C	A8	B4
D	D	1A	27	34	41	4E	5B	68	75	82	8F	9C	A9	B6	C3
E	E	1C	2A	38	46	54	62	70	7E	8C	9A	A8	B6	C4	D2
F	F	1E	2D	3C	4B	5A	69	78	87	96	A5	B4	C3	D2	E1

A-6 BINARY-CODED DECIMAL (BCD) CODE

The BCD system is a subset of the HD code and represents decimal numbers by the following code:

Number	BCD Code	Number	BCD Code
0	0000	5	0101
1	0001	6	0110
2	0010	7	0111
3	0011	8	1000
4	0100	9	1011

For example, in this code $359_{(10)}$ would be, in BCD code,

$$0011{\blacktriangle}0101{\blacktriangle}1001$$

To find the decimal equivalent of a binary number, add the proper powers of 2 where there is a "1" coefficient. For example, binary 100111110 would be:

$$2^0 = 0, 2^1 = 2, 2^2 = 4, 2^3 = 8, 2^4 = 16, 2^5 = 32, \text{ and } 2^8 = 256$$

Thus, the final result is $310_{(10)}$.

To find the equivalent binary number for a decimal number, the decimal number is continuously divided by 2 and the remainder recorded in order. The binary numbers are the "1s" and "0s" arranged in reverse order as follows:

$$2) \underline{359}$$
$$179 = 1$$

$$2) \underline{22}$$
$$10 = 1$$

$$2) \underline{179}$$
$$89 = 1$$

$$2) \underline{11}$$
$$5 = 1$$

$$2) \underline{89}$$
$$44 = 1$$

$$2) \underline{5}$$
$$2 = 0$$

$$2) \underline{44}$$
$$22 = 0$$

$$2) \underline{2}$$
$$1 = 1$$

Therefore, the binary equivalent is equal to $359_{(10)} = 10110111_{(2)}$.

A-6.1 A 6-bit Alphanumeric Code

Two to the sixth power is 64; thus, a 6-bit code can represent all the numerics (0 to 9) and all the letters (A to Z). For simple printouts this code is sufficient, but it does not allow for both capitals and lowercase letters. The numbers 0 to 9 require 4 bits, and the letters A to Z require an additional 2 bits. Examples of a typical 6-bit code are shown in Table A-6.

A-6.2 Alphanumeric Codes [Extended Binary-Coded Decimal Interchange Code (EBCDIC)]

In Chapter 7 and earlier in Chapter 3 we covered both serial and the present standard parallel codes; however, for devices that process only alphanumerics the minimum number of bits is 6, which provides

TABLE A-6

1.	000000	A.	110001	J.	100001	S.	010010
2.	000010	B.	110010	K.	100010	T.	010011
3.	000011	C.	110011	L.	100011	U.	010100
4.	000100	D.	110100	M.	100100	V.	010101
5.	000101	E.	110101	N.	100101	W.	010110
6.	000110	F.	110110	O.	100110	X.	010111
7.	000111	G.	110111	P.	100111	Y.	011000
8.	001000	H.	111000	Q.	101000	Z.	011001
9.	001001	I.	111001	R.	101001		
0.	001010						

Table A-7

EBCDIC Code

EBCDIC	Bit Configuration	Hex	EBCDIC	Bit Configuration	Hex	EBCDIC	Bit Configuration	Hex	EBCDIC	Bit Configuration	Hex
NULL	0000 0000		b (blank)	0100 0000	40		1000 0000			1100 0000	C0
	0000 0001			0100 0001		a	1000 0001	81	A	1100 0001	C1
	0000 0010			0100 0010		b	1000 0010	82	B	1100 0010	C2
	0000 0011			0100 0011		c	1000 0011	83	C	1100 0011	C3
PF	0000 0100	04		0100 0100		d	1000 0100	84	D	1100 0100	C4
HT	0000 0101	05		0100 0101		e	1000 0101	85	E	1100 0101	C5
LC	0000 0110	06		0100 0110		f	1000 0110	86	F	1100 0110	C6
DEL	0000 0111	07		0100 0111		g	1000 0111	87	G	1100 0111	C7
	0000 1000		C	0100 1000		h	1000 1000	88	H	1100 1000	C8
	0000 1001			0100 1001	49	i	1000 1001	89	I	1100 1001	C9
	0000 1010		¢	0100 1010	4A		1000 1010			1100 1010	
	0000 1011		.	0100 1011	4B		1000 1011			1100 1011	
	0000 1100		<	0100 1100	4C		1000 1100			1100 1100	
	0000 1101		(	0100 1101	4D		1000 1101			1100 1101	
	0000 1110		+	0100 1110	4E		1000 1110			1100 1110	
	0000 1111		!	0100 1111	4F		1000 1111			1100 1111	
	0001 0000		&	0101 0000			1001 0000			1101 0000	D0
	0001 0001			0101 0001		j	1001 0001	91	J	1101 0001	D1
	0001 0010			0101 0010		k	1001 0010	92	K	1101 0010	D2
	0001 0011			0101 0011		l	1001 0011	93	L	1101 0011	D3
RES	0001 0100	14		0101 0100		m	1001 0100	94	M	1101 0100	D4
NL	0001 0101	15		0101 0101		n	1001 0101	95	N	1101 0101	D5
BS	0001 0110	16		0101 0110		o	1001 0110	96	O	1101 0110	D6
IDL	0001 0111	17		0101 0111		p	1001 0111	97	P	1101 0111	D7
	0001 1000			0101 1000		q	1001 1000	98	Q	1101 1000	D8
	0001 1001			0101 1001		r	1001 1001	99	R	1101 1001	D9
	0001 1010		!	0101 1010	5A		1001 1010			1101 1010	
	0001 1011		$	0101 1011	5B		1001 1011			1101 1011	
	0001 1100		*	0101 1100	5C		1001 1100			1101 1100	
	0001 1101		)	0101 1101	5D		1001 1101			1101 1101	
	0001 1110		;	0101 1110	5E		1001 1110			1101 1110	
	0001 1111		¬	0101 1111	5F		1001 1111			1101 1111	
	0010 0000		−	0110 0000	60		1010 0000			1110 0000	E0
	0010 0001		/	0110 0001	61		1010 0001			1110 0001	
	0010 0010			0110 0010		s	1010 0010	A2	S	1110 0010	E2
	0010 0011			0110 0011		t	1010 0011	A3	T	1110 0011	E3
BYP	0010 0100	24		0110 0100		u	1010 0100	A4	U	1110 0100	E4
LF	0010 0101	25		0110 0101		v	1010 0101	A5	V	1110 0101	E5
EOB	0010 0110	26		0110 0110		w	1010 0110	A6	W	1110 0110	E6
PRE	0010 0111	27		0110 0111		x	1010 0111	A7	X	1110 0111	E7
	0010 1000			0110 1000		y	1010 1000	A8	Y	1110 1000	E8
	0010 1001			0110 1001		z	1010 1001	A9	Z	1110 1001	E9
	0010 1010			0110 1010			1010 1010			1110 1010	
	0010 1011		,	0110 1011	6B		1010 1011			1110 1011	
	0010 1100		%	0110 1100	6C		1010 1100			1110 1100	
	0010 1101		_	0110 1101	6D		1010 1101			1110 1101	
	0010 1110		>	0110 1110	6E		1010 1110			1110 1110	
	0010 1111		?	0110 1111	6F		1010 1111			1110 1111	
	0011 0000			0111 0000			1011 0000		0	1111 0000	F0
	0011 0001			0111 0001			1011 0001		1	1111 0001	F1
	0011 0010			0111 0010			1011 0010		2	1111 0010	F2
	0011 0011			0111 0011			1011 0011		3	1111 0011	F3
PN	0011 0100	34		0111 0100			1011 0100		4	1111 0100	F4
RS	0011 0101	35		0111 0101			1011 0101		5	1111 0101	F5
UC	0011 0110	36		0111 0110			1011 0110		6	1111 0110	F6
EOT	0011 0111	37		0111 0111			1011 0111		7	1111 0111	F7
	0011 1000			0111 1000			1011 1000		8	1111 1000	F8
	0011 1001			0111 1001	79		1011 1001		9	1111 1001	F9
	0011 1010		:	0111 1010	7A		1011 1010			1111 1010	
	0011 1011		#	0111 1011	7B		1011 1011			1111 1011	
	0011 1100		@	0111 1100	7C		1011 1100			1111 1100	
	0011 1101		'	0111 1101	7D		1011 1101			1111 1101	
	0011 1110		=	0111 1110	7E		1011 1110			1111 1110	
	0011 1111		"	0111 1111	7F		1011 1111			1111 1111	

2^6 (64 combinations) or enough to accommodate numbers, capital letters, punctuation, and special symbols. The general code now used almost universally is ASC II, which, in addition, has many control characters. It is basically a 7-bit code with parity. There is also another 7-bit code with somewhat similar characteristics, but it has fewer symbols coded than ASC II. This is called the *BCD interchange code*, or *BCDIC*, a more expanded code that contains capital letters, punctuation, symbols, control characters, and even lower-case letters. This is an 8-bit code (9 with parity) and is called the *extended binary-coded decimal interchange code*, or *EBCDIC*. This code is illustrated by Table A-7, originally a magnetic tape code.

RATING COMPUTERS ON PERFORMANCE:
Kilo-operations per second (KOPs)

One of the ways to rate a computer is to explore its operating speed for solving a particular problem, typical to its expected operation. This process involves comparing the speed at which one or more computers perform a standard program. Usually, a standard set of instructions multiplied by their percentage of occurrence is added and the reciprocal computed to get a relative KOPs figure.

As an example, the following is provided:

• Transfers from memory	1 microsecond at	20%
• Additions	2.5 microseconds at	10%
• Double-precision multiplies	12.5 microseconds at	5%
• Transfer to memory	1 microsecond at	40%
• Table look-up	12 microseconds at	5%
• Address modification	2 microseconds at	10%
• Miscellaneous	5 microseconds at	10%
		100%

The calculations involve multiplication of the times by the percentages, adding, and taking the reciprocal, or:

$$
\begin{array}{rcl}
1 \times .2 &=& .2 \\
2.5 \times .1 &=& .1 \\
12.5 \times .05 &=& .625 \\
1 \times .4 &=& .4 \\
12.0 \times .05 &=& .6 \\
2 \times .1 &=& .2 \\
5 \times .1 &=& .5 \\
\hline
&& 2.625
\end{array}
$$

Then taking the reciprocal, we have:

$$1/2.625 = .381$$

Multiplying this by 1×10^6, we have:

$$381,000, \text{ or } 381 \text{ KOPs}$$

This is a reasonably fast computer. A computer's KOPs is a function of its basic internal clocking rate, the instruction mix, and whether—the addressing of memory is via a separate bus—that is, separate from the data bus—or via the same bus. Separate buses permit faster operation. If the same bus is used for both functions, the addressing and data flow occur in sequence. For computers like the 8086, Z8000, where addressing and data flow are separated, these are slower than a 4-bit slice processor.

Index